Royal Marines 1955–1957

Royal Marines 1955–1957

♦

A NATIONAL SERVICE ADVENTURE

INCLUDES SUEZ CANAL CONFLICT

R.H. *Lofthouse*
Marine *132049*

iUniverse, Inc.
New York Lincoln Shanghai

Royal Marines 1955–1957
A NATIONAL SERVICE ADVENTURE

Copyright © 2007 by R. H. Lofthouse

All rights reserved. No part of this book may be used or reproduced by any means, graphic, electronic, or mechanical, including photocopying, recording, taping or by any information storage retrieval system without the written permission of the publisher except in the case of brief quotations embodied in critical articles and reviews.

iUniverse books may be ordered through booksellers or by contacting:

iUniverse
2021 Pine Lake Road, Suite 100
Lincoln, NE 68512
www.iuniverse.com
1-800-Authors (1-800-288-4677)

The views expressed in this work are solely those of the author and do not necessarily reflect the views of the publisher, and the publisher hereby disclaims any responsibility for them.

ISBN: 978-0-595-43589-0 (pbk)
ISBN: 978-0-595-87915-1 (ebk)

Printed in the United States of America

This book is dedicated to the Royal Marines

Contents

Foreword ix
Preface xi
Acknowledgements xiii
Introduction xv
HERE WE GO xvii
BECOMING A MARINE 1
HERE WE GO AGAIN 5
NEARLY A MARINE 9
COMMANDO 14
MUD AND GUTS 18
CYPRUS 24
MALTA 30
PORT SAID 39
AMPHIBIOUS LANDING 44
PORT SAID SECURE 51
'A' TROOPS OBJECTIVES 52
JARDINIERRE SQUARE 57
CEASEFIRE 59
RETURN TO CYPRUS 65

FATEFUL AMBUSH 73
RETURN TO MALTA 78
NAPOLI 84
HOMEWARD VOYAGE 87
DEMOB 90
MEMORIES 93

Foreword

"We were scared, to say the least, but the next thing that happened almost made us mess our pants! As we were passing in-between the cruisers, they broadsided and the noise nearly blew our eardrums out. It was unbelievable stuff. As they fired these broadsides the recoil of their huge guns lifted the cruisers about ten metres back. What a fright! I looked at Jimmy Shade and he looked at me—we were both as white as sheets. Is this real or is it a nightmare? Still, the assault crafts kept on going. We could see just over the craft's side and saw the beach huts that were all now on fire, some even exploding."

This is a fast-paced first-hand account of the experiences of a young Royal Marine who fought in the battle for the liberation of the Suez Canal, and describes the heart-warming camaraderie that bound together national servicemen and officers alike. The book is dedicated to all those who died serving their country during the years 1955 to 1957. Reading this true-life adventure of comrades in arms, of self-sacrifice, chilling encounters with death and heroic exploits, one can have no doubt that Marine Lofthouse 132049 is one of those who constitute the salt of the earth, to whom we in the free world owe a profound debt.

Charles Muller, MA (Wales) Ph.D (Lond), D.Litt (OFS), D.Ed (SA)
Diadem Books
www.diadembooks.com

Preface

This book is written from memory and I apologise to anyone whose name appears in this book if I have spelt his or her name incorrectly. I do hope that everyone I met on this adventure has done well in life and, hopefully, is still around and enjoying good health.

The reason this book was written is due to conversations in my local club and various other people suggesting "You should write a book, Lofty, it will sell like hot cakes!"—or words to that effect. There will be some things or events that I have not included, simply because I did not recall them. I'm sure some of the marines who were on this two-year adventure will remember some of these incidents or events. This book is really dedicated to all of the marines, be it squaddies, N.C.O.s or officers who were lucky enough to be in 40 commando on the dates November 1955 to November 1957, the specific dates of this adventure, be it national service or regular service. Sadly, but proudly, the dedication includes all those who died serving their country at this time. My sincere commiserations go out to their families.

By penning this book, I hope to come in contact with some of the marines who would like this to happen. I'll never forget the camaraderie that was so strong amongst us. I have no hesitation in recommending to anyone who wishes to join the forces, to join the Royal Marines. It's a great way to see foreign places and there is never a dull moment, as you are forever on the move. I sincerely hope the readers of this book will enjoy it for what it is—a true-life adventure.

Read on!

R. H. Lofthouse, Marine 132049

Acknowledgements

Sincere thanks are due to Charles Muller of Diadem Books for his advice and help in putting this book together.

Introduction

I left school on a Friday afternoon at 15 years of age, starting work as an apprentice bricklayer on the following Monday. Jobs were easier to get back in 1950. I completed my apprenticeship in November 1955. My call-up papers arrived the same day I became a fully-fledged bricklayer. I had to report at an enlistment office (for national service) in Newcastle-on-Tyne. Everything seemed to happen fast those days. I was one of 40 lads at the enlistment office that morning; some of them were trying to get deferred for various reasons. I, and most of the other lads, knew we could not get a deference as we were 21 years of age and it seemed that the services were somewhat desperate to enlist as many as possible.

We were given a choice of which service we would like to join—Army, Navy or Royal Air Force. Enlistment officers and N.C.O.s were present to advise the recruitment. Seeing as I could not swim, it seemed commonsense to join the army, but I had this thing in my head that said join the navy and learn to swim! When the N.C.O.s gave us the forms to fill in I ticked the square next to Royal Navy. A navy rep came to me with my completed form and suggested I should enlist as a soldier on board a fleet ship. I asked him what he meant and he explained that the navy probably had no vacancies and suggested I should enlist as a royal marine on board a ship.

Being as green as grass, I signed the form. Even though I was only 5'4" tall, I had been persuaded to join the Royal Marines.

After the recruitment was finished I found out that I was the only one who had joined the marines; most had joined the army, some the fleet air arm and the rest the air force. When I got on the bus to go home I felt as though I had been press-ganged into joining the marines. When I got home and told my mother and father what had happened, they just said what they always said: "You've made your bed so you'll just have to lie in it."

In other words, just get on with it and do your best. Two weeks later I received instructions to report to Lympstone Marine Barracks in Devon on a certain date and a certain time.

In-between the recruitment day and the day I had to report, we had to have a medical which was nothing really, just heart checks, eyesight and simple tests. The paperwork for these tests had to be handed over to the sick bay doctor when arriving at Lympstone. At the time of my call-up I was engaged to be married but nothing had been arranged, so it looked as though the marriage would have to wait.

HERE WE GO

On the day I had to report, I was seen off by my fiancée at Newcastle Central Station on route to Temple Meads Station at Bristol. From there I had to catch a train to Exeter. The train arrived at Exeter on time.

On the platform a royal marine sergeant and two corporals were calling names out and forming the recruits up in lines to march off to trucks parked outside the station. By the time we reached Temple Meads station the train had picked up about 20 of us at different stations on route. By the time we reached Exeter there were about 40 of us. The sergeant had the list of those he was supposed to collect and when he roll called, everyone was there. Standing in line on the platform, one could sense the military organisation kicking in.

Into the trucks we climbed and off we went to Lympstone camp. I loved adventures, and I was about to embark on a 2-year national service adventure. This adventure I will never forget for as long as I live.

When we arrived at Lympstone it soon became clear to me that I was not going to be a marine on a ship. As we disembarked at the gates of Lympstone Royal Marine Corps barracks, we looked around and saw the assault course on the banks of the river Exe. There were some groans when we realised we were going to be attempting this course soon. The sergeant reported to the guardhouse while the corporals assembled the 40 or so of us into marching ranks.

When the sergeant came back, he instructed the corporals to march us to certain billets further into the camp. We passed the NAAFI, some marines doing a speed march and a squad of marines who'd had their passing out parade and were off on leave before being posted. We were their replacement squad, all national service, here for 13 weeks royal marine training and 4-weeks commando training at Bickleigh, Devon.

We did not realise this until the next afternoon. Everyone was laughing at us as we tried to march in step in our civilian clothes and carrying our essentials, which we had been instructed to bring. I was really pleased when we reached the billets. Upon reaching the billets, the sergeant designated 10 to each billet. Four billets were allocated to this new squad. Each billet had 10 beds plus a 6' x 4' cabinet next to each bed. It also had a room at the entrance where the billet corporal was housed. There were two coal stoves to each billet with the flue going up to and through the roof; these were jet black and it looked like the stoves and flues had been blackened every day. There was also a fire bucket next to each cabinet, half filled with sand. These were also blackened.

It was just about dark when we reached the billets. It was winter and five weeks till Christmas, 1955. That night I never slept a wink—I felt like a boy in a man's world. At 06:30 the next day the reveille sounded followed by the corporal shouting for us to get up. We were shown where the ablutions were and told in no uncertain terms that we had to be back at the billet straight after breakfast.

Breakfast was at 7 a.m. in the dining hall. I thought the breakfast was okay although some lads didn't go a bundle on it! When we were washed, shaved and fed, we all returned to our billet. At about 07:45 the corporal came in and said, "Stand by your beds." We did this just as the sergeant came in. We were instructed what to do with the bedclothes (how to do your bed up), given a key for the locker next to the bed and told, in no uncertain terms, that the billet had to be spotless or we would be on a charge. This included blackening the stoves, flues, buckets, etc. The sergeant and the officer would be inspecting the billets every morning at 07:45, we were told. We were then instructed to form up outside and then marched up to the quartermaster's stores to be kitted out with boots, socks, training clothes, berets, etc. Our dress uniforms were to be dealt with later in the week. We were allowed back to the billets to try everything on. There was very little that didn't fit—the quartermaster knew his job. The morning was over by the time all this had happened. In the afternoon we were all ordered into the gym and told to sit on the floor. The camp commander then put us in the picture, telling us that there would be 13 weeks training at Lympstone followed by 4-weeks commando training at Bickleigh. He then told us we would do 4-weeks training and then be allowed a week's leave at Christmas (1955). He then asked, "Are there any questions?"—but before anyone could put up his hand to ask, he said "Carry on sergeant" and left the hall. The sergeant then asked the corporals to show us around the camp (i.e. the assault course, the parade ground, the NAAFI and all the areas for practising and learning weaponry). It was then suppertime and back to the billets. We were told that the NAAFI was out of bounds until further notice; we could use the shop to buy boot polish and other necessities, but that was all.

Squad at beginning of training

November 1955 at Lympstone, Devon

At the beginning of training we were known as 'sproggs'. At the finish of the 13 weeks Marine training we became Marines. At the end of the training at Bickleigh and Dartmoor we then became Marine Commando's. The drill sergeant, to our right, was really hard but got us into shipshape fashion.

BECOMING A MARINE

The next 4 weeks consisted of drill in the mornings (learning how to march, salute and presenting arms, etc). It was midwinter and bitterly cold in the mornings. A couple of times a squaddy would faint with the cold; he would be revived, given approximately 10 minutes break and then put back into the drill. The drill sergeant was a hard man and informed us that every one of us had to be up to scratch or we would have to do the whole drill again.

Pretty soon we all realised we had to help the weaker ones along or we would have to repeat everything again. The mornings were really cold but by the time we had completed the drills (attention, slope arms, present arms, stand at ease, salute properly) we were lathered!

When everything started to fall into place one could feel the rhythm and it became natural. We were told to salute only officers, not N.C.O.s as some of us were prone to do.

I remember one lad who could not keep in step when marching; they soon cured him by making him double around the parade ground with his rifle above his head. After four or five times of this treatment he quickly learnt how to march in step.

The afternoons were taken up by the whole squad having to master the assault course and weapon training after showering and changing into clean denims.

The assault course consisted of ditches, vertical walls, rope riggings, two feet diameter pipes, low walls, etc. This assault course had to be done at the double (running), crawling through the pipes (approx eight feet long), climbing up the rope riggings, jumping down the other side, running at and jumping the low walls, clearing the ditches and any other obstacle, to end up having to climb a seven-foot high vertical wall, landing into water on the other side. This had to be done in a certain time by everyone in the squad. If someone lagged and looked like taking the squad time over the limit, the rest of the squad had to re-track and help whoever it was so we did not have to do it again. One lad was not athletic enough to keep up and was always last. He was always coaxed and helped by the rest of us; he had actually joined the marines but ended up in the medical corp after we passed out of our training.

Every time we did the assault course we could see the death slide and wondered when it would be our turn to attempt it. I found that the rope rigging was always the hardest obstacle—it was like one step forward and two steps backwards.

The vertical wall was hard to climb but once you jumped and grabbed the top, it was just sheer strength and determination that got you over.

After the assault course, the afternoons were completed by taking lessons on cleaning weapons, stripping them down and reassembling them. The weapons we used were rifles, mortars, sten guns, bren guns, etc. By the time lights out came we were all dog-tired and slept like logs, except for the lad who we were consistently helping. He kept praying and talking in his sleep. Clearly he had picked the wrong mob to be in. He was a big lad and we could not understand why he had not taken to it. We later found out that his father was a vicar; indeed, it was his father who got him transferred to the medical corp for the rest of his national service after we passed out.

The first four weeks were physically hard but we had Christmas leave to look forward to. We had by now been measured and had our dress uniforms, which we went on leave wearing. We went on leave knowing that when we returned to Lympstone we had the death slide and assault course to conquer. No one was looking forward to that. However, we left Lympstone in our dress uniforms feeling very fit and able, looking forward to seeing our families and friends.

When I arrived home in my uniform, my mother cried. "What's the matter?" I asked. I thought I looked okay in my navy blue with red trims, white belt, red and blue cap and black boots you could see your own face in!

"She's crying because she's proud of you," my father said.

I had a look in the mirror and boy, did I look something! In that one week of leave I saw a lot of my fiancée and had some great beer sessions with my mates.

When the week's leave was up I got dressed in my uniform and went to my local club for a final drink. My train was due at 9.30 p.m. and I had to be on it.

Somebody put me on the train drunk. Luckily there were a few empty carriages so I slept for a while. When I woke up there were two other marines sitting opposite me. They must have got on at York. We were in the same squad so everything was all right. By the time we arrived at Templemeads, Bristol, a few more marines had boarded the train. Again these were from the same squad. We boarded the train from Bristol to Plymouth, got off at Exeter and climbed into probably the same trucks that had picked us up originally. They had been waiting for the connection.

AUTHOR
Marine 132049 Lofthouse

This photograph was taken at Lympstone Barracks, December 1955, after dress uniforms were tailored and issued. River Exe is in the background.

HERE WE GO AGAIN

A lot of the lads weren't looking forward to getting back to Lympstone. I was slightly excited. I knew that the assault course and the death slide would still be there and I was looking forward to conquering them.

It was New Year's Eve when we arrived at Lympstone marine barracks, late afternoon and getting dark. We checked in at the guardhouse and made our way down to the billets. There were only a couple of us missing.

When we looked at the work sheet for the following week we saw that it was nearly the same schedule as before—drill and lectures in the morning and physical training (assault course) in the afternoon. On the bottom of the list was 'death slide'. Everybody moaned—even I was sceptical!

That night we celebrated New Year's Eve, drinking tea or cocoa and bulling the billet up. By this time the two lads who were missing had arrived so we were back to a full squad ready for what was in store, or so we thought.

New Year's Day came and went. We had no money so there wasn't much we could do except stay in the billet, make sure the place was spotless and just sit around talking about anything. I was now Marine Lofthouse no. 132049, a number you remember for as long as you live.

At that time, early 1956, the Cyprus crisis was in the headlines, something was happening in Belize and President Nasser of Egypt was just starting to draw attention to himself. We talked about where we would be posted; the three places in the headlines did not appeal but we knew we would end up at one of those venues.

Malta was in our thoughts, but we knew Malta was just a staging post for the Middle East. The vicar's son said he wouldn't go to any of these places mentioned; he was right, but it was in an ignominious way, being transferred eventually.

The big Cockney lad said he couldn't wait to get to Cyprus and flush out general George Grivas and Archbishop Makarias; he would sort out Cyprus when he got there. What a big-mouthed braggart we all thought—none of us liked him. However, we were in the same squad and had no choice but to listen to him; he was about 6'2" so I just listened and said nothing.

Lights out sounded and the corporal popped in and informed us to be by our beds in the morning.

The next thing we knew was being woken up by Reveille the next morning. Washed, shaved and dressed in our denim uniforms, we shot up to the dining hall for breakfast. Feeling very hungry, I wolfed mine down, ate one of the lads' breakfast as he wasn't hungry and I felt great.

We made our way back to the billet, made sure everything was spic and span, then formed up next to our beds ready for inspection.

Right on cue the officer and sergeant arrived, inspected the billets and left. The corporal formed us up in marching ranks outside and marched us to the parade ground. It was snowing slightly, bitterly cold and icy. It was noticeable that we were in-step, all in the same frame of mind.

"Form up!" the drill sergeant shouted.

"Stand at ease." We all did this at the same time, one noise.

"Atten-tion!" shouted the drill sergeant; again, only one noise.

"Slope arms." We were right on form.

"Present arms!" Right on again, we were there, a unit; the drill sergeant had succeeded with us.

"Slope arms. Move to the right in threes." That was the next order.

Off we went, in perfect step. Even the vicar's son was in-step. The timing was perfect; it was implanted in our heads—we were as one, uniformed robots. Everything was becoming easy and very military. The drill sergeant never praised us, just kept shouting orders.

When the drill was finished we all said (when we were at ease) that we had enjoyed that. Even the weapon training seemed to be falling into place—we had been brainwashed and were glad of it.

We still had to conquer the death slide.

The assault, or obstacle course, as some lads called it, was on the side of the river Exe that flowed alongside the camp to Exmouth. With the snow melt from the moors it was at full bore every day in the winter of 1955/56 and, boy, was the water cold! Luckily the assault course ran alongside and not across the river. The views from the highest part of the camp were fantastic; it actually was a lovely place to be at, even though we were training relentlessly. Once one became really fit, one began to appreciate the surroundings—but the death slide loomed ominously.

One afternoon after we had successfully completed the assault course, the sergeant instructed the corporals to assemble the squad at the death slide site. We were marched at the double and stood at ease so the sergeant could explain what the drill was to complete this obstacle named the 'death slide'.

There was a very tall tree about thirty metres in height, trimmed up to about twenty-five metres with scaffolding around the bare trunk up to approximately twenty-two metres. There was a platform at twenty metres, about two by two metres, with a handrail to three sides; the fourth side was open.

The tree trunk was approximately two feet in diameter at this height, with the platform all around it. About two metres above the platform was a two-inch diameter rope tied to the tree, secured so that it wouldn't slip. This rope stretched all the way to the ground, about fifty metres away towards the assault course, through the open part of the platform. The rope, of course, was taut. On the platform was a bucket of water and a dozen toggles. The idea was to loop the toggles over the slide rope and slide all the way down to the ground. Toggles were 2ft lengths of rope with a wooden handle fixed to each end. The sergeant had to be on the platform to instruct us how to go on. Two corporals would be at the bottom of the slide rope to make sure we landed properly.

The sergeant emphasised the fact that the toggles had to be dipped into the bucket of water before being looped over the slide rope. This was to stop rope burn as we slid down to the ground.

First of all we had to climb up the scaffolding to reach the platform. The sergeant would be on the platform to make sure everything was done correctly. First up the scaffold was the Cockney. There was only one recruit allowed on the platform at a time. The next recruit had to be at the edge of the platform ready to step on when the previous recruit had slid down the death slide. I'll never forget what happened next. This recruit in front of me climbed on to the platform. I was at platform level ready to climb on. The sergeant said to him, "Pick the toggle up and dip the toggle into the bucket of water, loop the toggle over the 2" slide rope and just step off the platform—the two corporals will make sure you land properly." The recruit picked up the toggle, took hold of it with both hands, dipped it into the bucket of water, raised the toggle above his head and stepped off the platform. The sergeant shouted before he stepped: "Stop, loop the toggle over the slide rope!"—but it was too late. He had forgotten to throw one handle of the toggle over the slide rope, then grab it and step off. He fell like a stone, twenty metres on to a grassy bank. The sergeant was down the scaffold like a shot. The two corporals also ran to the lad and so did every one of the squad who were still at ground level. When they got to him he just got up as though nothing had happened. The corporal took him to the sick bay but apart from bruises he was okay. We carried on with the death slide, the sergeant making sure we all got the toggle over the slide rope. When we had done it a few times it got to be easy as long as the sergeant's instructions were adhered to. When we were finished that afternoon we got back to the billets and there was the recruit who had fallen, sitting as large as life. He said he was a bit sore but that was all. How he had come through that without breaking anything I'll never know.

NEARLY A MARINE

The next weeks were much the same as before, concentrating on fitness, learning how to fire rifles, mortars, bren guns, sten guns, etc. A couple of times a week we were taken to the firing range somewhere near Plymouth. The range was on the coast so we were firing at the targets and if we missed, the rounds just went into the sea. I was pretty good with a .303 rifle and enjoyed it. The weather was still diabolical but spring was on its way—surely the weather would change for the better.

We were now two thirds of the way through our royal marine training. I was lucky enough to be selected for the camp football team and was excused duties on a Wednesday and Saturday afternoon. The NAAFI was now in bounds for us, but we never had enough money to spend on ale. One night in the billet we decided to pool all the money each recruit had left after buying their necessities, add it up and divide it by 8 pence (the price of a pint of Scrumpy). It was then divided into three pints per man; the number of men was decided by the number of pints the money would buy. Then we drew the names out of a hat. If it was five men wanted, then it was the first five names out of the hat. The next week those names were not put into the hat, therefore allowing everybody a chance to have a good drink. Not all of the recruits agreed to donate so they weren't included.

I was lucky enough to be drawn out first time. I'd heard a lot about this Scrumpy (cider) but just laughed at the other lads in the camp who said it was a very strong drink. The following Saturday night we made our way up to the NAAFI and booked a turn on the snooker table and bought our first pint of Scrumpy. The first pint went down a treat. It tasted like rough apple juice—which, in fact, it was!

Our turn to play snooker came as we ordered our second pint; the marine serving behind the NAAFI bar warned us that the Scrumpy would hit us really hard if we drank it too fast.

One of the lads set the balls up on the snooker table and we took our turns trying to pot the balls. One lad decided the Scrumpy was too strong for him and he left after one and a half pints. We just laughed. After two pints everything seemed to be in a haze, like a surreal feeling. The bar tender had to be coaxed into serving us a third pint. Half way down the third pint none of us could hit the balls properly—the Scrumpy was taking effect! The next thing I knew a recruit was on the snooker table kicking the balls into the pockets, or trying to. The bar tender came over and told us to leave or he would have to call the camp guards to throw us out. We did as he asked and made our way to the billets, singing, shouting and kicking things over. I can't for the life of me remember going into the billet. The next thing I knew was waking up with a terribly bad headache, dry mouth and aching all over. I put my feet on to the floor and realised my feet were in about a half inch of water. I couldn't work it out why I was now standing in this water. The other lads in the billet started waking up and gave every one of us who had been out on the Scrumpy a right rollicking. Apparently we'd entered the billet and had started filling the buckets up with water and had been throwing the water all over the billet. The place was in a mess—wet sand, water, tins of boot polish, boots, belts and you name it, it was all scattered around.

Just then the corporal who had been out of camp that night put his head around the door and said, "Jesus Christ, get this billet cleaned up before I come back or you will all be on a charge!" Luckily it was a Sunday and neither the officer nor the sergeant would be around.

We got called some names that day but we got the billet back to the way it was. When the corporal came back he said that if the sergeant had come we would all have been charged. He was okay and forgot all about it. That was the last pint of Scrumpy for me. The system of pooling money for Scrumpy wasn't repeated.

Whilst at Lympstone camp we did a few manoeuvres on Exmoor. What a desolate place that is in the winter! Every time we returned to camp we had to have a shower and change into fresh clothes. We never looked forward to these outings as we were practically always up to the eyes in mud and soaked to the skin.

It was coming up to the end of our training at Lympstone and we were looking forward to our passing out parade. I've never been fitter in my life and felt great. Some of the other recruits felt the same, but there were always one or two moaners. Our passing out date was the third week in February, 1956. The weather was still wintry.

The night before our passing out parade we were blackening our boots so you could see your face in them, making sure our dress uniforms were immaculate, our belts 'blancoed' properly and our white gloves clean. Our caps, too, had to be spot on. Cap badges shining, epaulets in order, in fact, we had to look like a million dollars.

Before the parade we were inspected by the drill sergeant and corporal and passed ready to go. We also had to make sure our .303 rifles were clean as they would be inspected on parade as well. It was time to go to the shed on the parade ground to be ready for when the camp commander came. The shed was a huge, roofed building with one side open. This is where we drilled when it was raining. The rostrum was set up next to the camp flagpole. The C.O. arrived and had a few words of encouragement for us, but his last words were, "Get it right or it will have to be done again the next week!" The drill sergeant and corporal also encouraged us and told us to give 100% concentration.

The C.O. stepped on to the rostrum with the squad officer and weapon-training instructors (sergeants and corporals) at the side of the rostrum. The drill sergeant called us to form up on the white line, space ourselves with our arms outstretched touching the shoulder of the marine next to us. We were then called to attention, slope arms, right turn, by the right, quick march, and off we went as one unit.

Left turn, halt, order arms, stand at ease, attention, left turn, move to the left in threes, quick march, squad halt! We then had our rifles inspected. After this we had to do the slow march. Drill went on for one hour and, I swear, we didn't put a foot wrong. At the end of this parade we had to march past the C.O. "Eyes right!"—then into the shed where we were made to stand at ease. The C.O. had a word with the drill sergeant and said "Well done, lads!" as he went past and back to the officers' quarters. The drill sergeant then addressed us, saying we had passed but he thought it wasn't 100%. The corporal afterwards told us that the sergeant always said those words to every squad who passed. The notice from the C.O. was pinned onto the notice board and had 8 out of 10. I thought we were great, and we had the rest of the day off.

The following Sunday saw us at Exeter Cathedral. We were taken to Exeter in trucks wearing our dress uniforms. We formed up into marching order about a quarter of a mile from the Cathedral, then marched to about 100 yards from the Cathedral. From there, after a short break, we were slow marched up to and into the Cathedral in front of crowds of spectators who applauded as we marched past. Apparently this happened with every squad who passed out at Lympstone. After the service, we formed up outside and we marched back to where the trucks were waiting to take us back to camp.

Whilst playing for the camp football team I met some great people in the camp team and around the Exmoor area at places such as Crediton, Buddleigh Salterton, Sidmouth, Tavistock, Tiverton, Topsham, Bickleigh, Honiton and various other places. I wouldn't have missed it for the world. We were 100 percent fit, and when you're fit everything seems to be enjoyable. What a lovely part of the country Exmoor is!

Passing out photograph at the end of Marine training at Lympstone, Devon

Squad officer seated in centre. Drill sergeant and drill corporal to his left with weapons sergeant and corporal to his right. Marine 132049 Lofthouse top row end to officers' right. Jimmy Shade two in, and Jock Miller end of top row to officers' left.

COMMANDO

We had finished our royal marine training. Next was Bickleigh and four weeks of hell. The regular marines did double what we had done, 26 weeks in all. When they went to Bickleigh, they did 8 weeks commando training. We were national service, so we did half the time. It seemed they needed numbers in the marines, and national service lads filled the bill. Spring was in the air so we were a bit happier. We were still in Lympstone camp and made the journey to Bickleigh by trucks, returning to Lympstone after the training at Bickleigh. Same billets had to be spotless. We were somewhat estranged from Lympstone, even though we were billeted there. The next batch of national servicemen had arrived and we were senior to them. We still had the use of the dining hall for breakfast and supper and could still use the NAAFI. I could still play football for the camp team, but we knew that as soon as the training at Bickleigh was finished we would be posted abroad.

The commando training at Bickleigh was to be exceptionally tough. We were taken by trucks to the assembly point at Bickleigh, disembarked and moved into the specific places where we were to move out and engage in the drills or manoeuvres that were on the agenda.

These sorties were done either in Bickleigh forest or Dartmoor. The ones in Bickleigh were forced four-mile and seven-mile speed marches with full kit and rifles, with the corporals and sergeants screaming at us as we moved along, shouting at some lads who lagged a bit to get on with it or the whole squad would have to do it again. We practically dragged some people along; it wasn't the same lads all the time, but we all had our off days. These speed marches had to be done at four miles in something like twenty-four minutes, seven miles in something like forty-five minutes, all wearing hobnail boots and full kit, which was backpack, ammunition pouch, water bottle and .303 rifle. Boy, were we knackered when we finished! Then in Bickleigh forest (it certainly seemed like a forest) we had to scale quarries, abseil down them, climb back up if we made a mess of the abseiling and do it again until we got it right—again, with sergeants and corporals screaming at us. Then there was a death slide across the river Exe. The river was approximately twenty yards wide and about two feet deep. The death slide went from tree to tree across the river and we had to drop off the slide just before the bank on the other side. If you were lucky you stayed upright; if you weren't you got soaked and had to carry on as if nothing had happened. There was another rope across the river that we had to straddle and crawl over to the other side. This one was really something: first you had to grab the rope, then pull yourself onto it, leave one leg dangling for balance, lie level on the rope and crawl across to the other side of the river. If you weren't doing it properly, the officer in charge would shake the rope so that you fell off, hanging on with both hands, and had to pull yourself back on to the rope. If you didn't hang on, you automatically fell into the river; you then had to start all over again, and at that time of the year the river was fast flowing and bitterly cold.

Nearly all the lads fell into the river at some time. Completing your day's training in cold, wet clothes was not very amusing so we had to make sure we got better at these training sessions. When it was time for a meal, a truck would arrive with hay boxes (metal food containers) and there was a thirty-minute break for food. The food was okay, I suppose, but by the time it was dished into your mess tin it was going cold so we had to gulp it down to feel any benefit. If you needed the toilet, it was behind some tree. (At last we had found out why we were told to carry toilet paper.) All this training was meant to mimic being in action. Just when we thought we had cracked it (after about two weeks), we were told that our next two weeks training was to be on Dartmoor. Odd days at Bickleigh we would be on the shooting range firing from different distances with the sten gun, .303 rifle and taking turns with the light machine gun (bren gun). Out on Exmoor on other odd days we would be learning how to use a mortar and how to throw handgrenades. This all seemed pretty straightforward until we started training on Dartmoor.

Our first training session on Dartmoor was somewhere near Okehampton. It was the first time we wore helmets. Previously we had trained wearing the Blue Beret. These helmets were to become a hinder to us. When we were dropped off the trucks we had to march to where the training was to start. On arriving we noticed that the training staff were not our usual ones. Most of them were six feet tall or over and built like outhouses (for want of a better word). The last part of the march was done at double time (running), and the ground was getting softer and wetter. When we reached our rendezvous (somewhere near High Willhays) we knew we were pretty high up on the moor. It was bitterly cold and wet; when you moved you could feel yourself sinking about four inches into the ground.

We were sorted into groups for bren gun training. A bren group consisted of a corporal, a bren gunner, his ammunition carrier and three or four riflemen. We were each given so many rounds of ammunition for our .303 rifles; the bren gunner was given ammo for the bren and his ammunition carrier had to carry six pouches of ammunition for the bren along with full kit and rifle with ammunition. All ammunition was blank; there was a feeling of dread amongst us. With all the extra weight we knew this was going to be hard. The objective was to capture this hill or tor, as they are called on Dartmoor. We each had to take our turn as bren gunner and ammunition carrier. The idea was to fire at this hilltop (marked with a flag) to keep the enemies' heads down while the rest of the squad advanced up the side of the tor to capture it. The bren group had to run about a hundred yards and when the order came to get down, you had to drop down immediately and start firing; as soon as you hit the ground, your backpack came up your back, hit the back of the helmet and pushed it down over your eyes. Seems stupid but that's how it was. After a few turns at this the truck arrived with the hay boxes. Needless to say, we were all knackered, having charged up the hill a few times, taken our turn at the bren group, being covered in mud and soaked to the skin. And all this time we were being screamed at by these giants of men! We devoured our food like starving animals and were not looking forward to the afternoon.

MUD AND GUTS

First bren group of the afternoon had myself as bren gunner. I had to carry the bren gun, which was heavy, and wait for the order, "Down!" Off we went, sinking approximately four inches into the boggy ground with every step, dog-tired. "Don't forget to fire as soon as you hit the ground, marine 132049!" screamed the officer, and "Down!" came the order, with the group squelching through the boggy ground. Down we flopped into the bog, up came my backpack to hit the back of my helmet, over my eyes went the helmet. I was firing with my helmet over my eyes! We couldn't hear anything because everybody else was firing the .303s at the target. I was still firing when I felt this tapping on top of my helmet. The ammunition carrier shouted for me to stop and when I did I realised it had been the officer with his stick tapping me on the helmet. I adjusted my helmet and saw him glaring down at me. "Do you realise you have just killed your own men advancing up the hill?" I looked up along the line of the barrel of the bren and saw, to my horror, that I had been firing at my own mates running up the hill.

"Luckily for you, marine 132049, the ammunition were blanks."

I then realised that all the ammunition had been blanks; it then became obvious that they wouldn't have dared issue live ammo in case a situation like this had happened. When asked the reason why I'd been firing in the wrong direction, I explained about the helmet coming over my eyes. It didn't matter how tight you fastened the strap, it still moved. I was given a lecture by a sergeant who was about 6'4" and never asked to be a bren gunner again.

This training on Dartmoor was savage, forever up to our ankles in mud and forever soaked to the skin.

I remember one occasion when we were put into groups of five or six, given a compass, given the coordinates of where our destination was and made to black up; and then driven to a certain point on the moor after dark and instructed to find our way back to rendezvous with the rest of the squad at a certain point and at a certain time. Needless to say, it was pitch black and we were not allowed torches. We got lost squelching through the moor bumping into everything you could imagine. We came across some old buildings on the moor and felt ourselves getting deeper into the ground. We eventually got to where the ground seemed to be harder around these buildings. The lad who had the compass got inside one of these derelict buildings and lit a match to check the coordinates and compass. To our delight he said we only had a couple of miles to go in an easterly direction.

After an hour we realised we were lost. We decided to wait till first light and move on then. As it was slowly starting to light up we heard voices. It was a sergeant and a couple of squaddies looking for our patrol. It was then that we noticed that our denims were white up to our knees. After joining up with the sergeant he explained that we had been walking in the lime pits at this lime quarry where the old buildings were. He got on the wireless and informed the powers that be that we had been found and that we looked like black and white minstrels. Can you imagine that? Black faces and hands, and white up to our knees! I *thought* my legs were warm that night!

We didn't get a rollicking for, as it turned out, we had been given the wrong destination point. We had a good laugh when we got back to the barracks. The next morning we went to breakfast with everyone calling us the minstrels. What a laugh! In the final week of our training at Bickleigh we did a lot of running and shooting at the end of the runs. We had to be finished by a certain time on a certain date. To finish that day we had to speed march to a point in Bickleigh, complete an assault course, run into the forest on the Exe, cross the river on a rope, straddling it, drop off the rope (hanging on with both hands), climb back on to the same rope, drop off on the other side of the Exe, and climb up to a death slide; then, glide down and run the last mile on to our shooting range, drop on to our bellies and fire our .303's five times at a target and then finish by running into the rendezvous. We were then told to get showered and form up outside the billets. As we had all started this marathon at five-minute intervals separately, we had to stand formed up and wait for the last ones to finish. I was as fit as a fiddle and felt great after showering and dressing into clean denims with my green beret perched on my head. When the squad was all present and correct, an officer addressed us and informed us that we would be told our postings and then we would be given three days' leave. The sergeant read the postings out and the majority of us were to be sent to Cyprus (Paphos). The vicar's son was transferred to the medical corps. Two went to Belize, about four were assigned to somewhere in Scotland and we were sent to Cyprus.

The ones sent to Cyprus (including myself) were informed that we would be joining 40 commando at Paphos. There were still three of us who couldn't swim. The sergeant bypassed this by saying "when you have to swim, you will swim!" I doubted this, but kept my mouth shut.

On our return from the three days leave we were garrisoned at Plymouth Royal Marine Barracks to wait for instructions to move abroad. After two or three days we were moved to an underground shelter on the Tottenham Court Road in London ready to fly to Malta first, and then on to Cyprus. We were in this claustrophobic shelter for two days and then driven by truck to a military airfield where we were embarked on to this aeroplane that looked as if it was ready to fall apart. I think it was a 'Hermes' troop plane. We were allocated the forward seats. I wondered why and soon realised the reason. The forward seats porthole windows looked on to the wings of the plane. When you looked out of the window the only things you could see were the wing and propelling engines. It was quite scary as you could see the rivets on the wing moving and oil coming out of the propellers and spreading across the wings. The officers and N.C.O.s were at the rear of the plane and had a better view of things. As I said to the other lads who couldn't swim, we were probably better off not looking at the sea as we were not swimmers. They agreed.

Celebrating our passing out.
Photo taken at Plymouth Barracks NAAFI.

Some of us enjoying a drink after our passing out parade. Shortly after this we were posted to Paphos on the Island of Cyprus. When this photograph was taken we had just finished 17 weeks of intensive training and were as fit as Lops. We were now 17 weeks into this National Service adventure. As you can see, the camaraderie was already there.

*"Trowbridge John", "Barnsley Pal", and myself
before posting to Cyprus. Taken on Plymouth Hoe.*

We landed in the dark at Malta airport and were told we had just landed to refuel and as soon as this was done we would continue to Cyprus. After approximately one hour we took off for Cyprus. Incidentally, just about two weeks before we finished our training, we were ushered into the large gym. A boxing ring had been erected and we all thought that this looked ominous. We were paired into similar heights and weights and told in no uncertain terms that we would be boxing each other, for 3 x 2 minute rounds. I was paired up with the lad who had stepped off the death slide and thought to myself, this should be easy—thinking that he must be thick and wouldn't know what to do in the ring! He was a quiet lad and had been conscripted along with his twin brother who was to box someone else. The bell went and I came out of my corner feeling great. I got the first punch into his face. He just looked at me and then proceeded to bamboozle me with lefts, rights, uppercuts and whatever other punches you could think of. The sergeant stopped the contest after one minute of the second round. I was really battered and knackered. The lad came up to me in my corner and apologised. I couldn't speak so I just winked at him. He, his brother and I, became good pals after this. It seems that he and his twin did not want to be separated whilst doing their national service so had joined the marines together. I later asked him what he was thinking when he stepped off the death slide. He just said the sergeant had confused him by shouting and bawling and he just automatically stepped off. He turned out to be a nice lad who was shy. He also said that he was a member of a boxing club somewhere in Leicester, where he learned boxing!

CYPRUS

It was early March 1956 when we touched down on the tarmac somewhere in Cyprus. When we disembarked from the plane the heat hit us and we were advised to cover our heads and arms 'till we got used to it'. On leaving the plane we were marched to trucks that would be taking us to Paphos on the South West coast of the island. The journey lasted about one and a half hours in sweltering heat. Luckily the trucks were covered in, as there was little shelter from the sun. From what we could see out of the rear of the truck the island looked a gorgeous place; it seemed to have everything—lovely beaches, forests, mountains and quiet villages with fantastic churches. We spent the next four months on this island and the job we had to do was help the local policemen at their stations, just in case terrorists took over, and go out on patrol to the extent of our limit. These patrols were supposed to look for terrorists or 'freedom fighters' as they called themselves. They were actually Greek Cypriots whose leader was a certain George Grivas. General George Grivas and Archbishop Makarias were apparently the instigators of this wave of terrorism. They wanted the island to be Greek and the Turks wanted the island to be Turkish. As it is now, the island is divided after the Turks invaded in 1974. We were there as a sort of peacekeeping force, or so they informed us. More like the island of Cyprus was a strategic staging post for the western allies, in case of trouble in the Middle East—my opinion, of course.

Our camp on the outskirts of Paphos was a tented one and was just the job really—cool under canvas throughout the day, and fairly warm at night. When we were off duty we were allowed to go into Paphos itself. We had to keep out of the no-go areas but could just amble about anywhere else. The local inhabitants were mostly Turks and they made us quite welcome at their markets and coffee shops. We got to know a lot of them by name. We used to play dominoes and cards with them in the coffee shops. We would be known to these people as 'The Englais.'

The Author constructing some furniture for our tent so we could play cards when off duty.

When we arrived in Cyprus, the squad had been whittled down to 33 marines. Two of the recruits had been taken out of the squad to be officers; the others had been discharged for health related reasons. The two who were taken to officer school were selected because one's father was a retired colonel and the other one's father was the printer or author of all the military weapons and training manuals used by the marines; the name of the latter was Russell Polden.

We were now in camp with regulars. There were another two or three Geordies amongst them and it didn't take long for us all to pal up. When in camp we had guard duty and fatigues to do. When we were on patrol we were out of camp for three or four days, sometimes bivouacked at observation posts overlooking valleys or forests. In our rations we would have tubes of condensed milk; we would put them together and boil it up in a mess tin—really tasty as a drink. Funny how one thinks up these things when everything is basic.

One patrol we were on was a walking patrol, in the heat of the midday sun, before we were brought to a halt and allowed to rest, lathered in sweat, in the shade against a high stone wall. One of the squad looked over the wall and said to me, "Hey Geordie, look what's over the wall." I looked through a gap in the wall and saw a field full of melons. One lad asked the officer and sergeant if it would be okay to have a melon; they looked around to see if everything was clear and nodded approval. The whole patrol was over the wall in a flash! There we were sitting in a field of melons, slicing them into segments and eating them. It was like nectar from the Gods—I'll never forget it. When we had our fill the patrol headed for camp.

When we were on police station duty it was for four or five days at a time. There were nearly always three Turkish policemen and a marine sergeant, corporal and four marines. We would be constantly on guard (taking turns) for 24 hours. There would be one policeman and one marine at lookout while the others were inside the station, either asleep, playing cards or listening to Turkish radio. The duties were done in 4-hour shifts. These stations were sited at strategic places outside of villages near Paphos. It was known that the terrorists were being supplied from some of the villagers and that's what we had to look out for.

One day whilst in camp the whole unit was called out to some part of the forest where apparently suspected terrorists were camped. There was always a list of terrorists' names and photos available and it seemed that a terrorist with a price on his head was in this group. His name was Constantinides and we went out to get him. They were surrounded and surrendered. Two of them had £5000 rewards on their heads. Constantinides was the leader and Efelthiou was the other £5000 terrorist; the others were unknown. They claimed they were bird watchers but the troop captain had their photographs so they were recognised. I don't know who got the reward, or where the money went, but someone was richer—probably the person who grassed them.

They were interrogated by Capt. Grant, Lieutenant Preston, and a Turkish Cypriot police sergeant who was the interpreter. The terrorists were taken away to Paphos police station and we were returned to barracks.

The next day we were all called out to the nearest village to where the terrorists were captured. The whole village was turned out on to a piece of flat land and all the males were interrogated as to who was supplying these terrorists. The local police were doing the interrogating while we just guarded the perimeter.

Captured Terrorists

*Top left: £5,000.00 on this man's head. His name was Constantinides.
Top right: Lieutenant Preston with sheet of terrorist photographs.
Bottom left: £5,000.00 on this man's head. His name was Efelthiou.
Bottom right: Captain 'Dicky' Grant with interrogator questioning terrorist Efelthiou.*

In Cyprus the Turks came across as good people with lovely bairns, but they were desperately poor. The Greeks seemed to abhor the fact that we were there. The Greeks wanted the British out of the country so they could take it over. Did this mean that they were terrorists, or were they freedom fighters? Should we have been there? Again, the strategic position of the island came to mind, as President Nasser was demanding a toll for every foreign ship that used the Suez Canal. It looked as though it was going to be fisticuffs with Nasser's Egypt soon. In the meantime the terrorist organisation of E.O.K.A. had to be dealt with. General George was as elusive as the scarlet pimpernel. Makarias was still spouting off and causing friction between governments and we were still on active service.

It was the middle of July 1956 and we were informed that we would be moving to Malta soon, to take part in some manoeuvres.

MALTA

We suspected something was up and guessed that it would be Egypt. We could only do as we were instructed so we embarked for Malta, arriving about the beginning of August. We were garrisoned at St. George's barracks, Sliema, just outside of the Maltese capital Valletta. The barracks were okay and we soon settled in. Malta is just a rocky island about seven miles wide by fourteen miles long at its widest and longest points. Its harbour was the most natural harbour I've ever seen—it was full of English warships of all kinds, plus local ships and boats. When we were off duty we used to hire a Garry (horse drawn carriage) to take us into Valletta. We had some great times in the bars, restaurants and down the famous gut. This gut was a kind of back street about ten feet wide; every other door was a bar and you could get anything you wanted down the gut, and I mean anything. The bars were always full of matelots, marines and other service personnel. A meal would cost a half crown, old money; it was always good stuff and plenty of it. We were warned about venereal diseases, and warned by films of young girls being on the lookout for marriage. We were reminded of what we had back home and advised not to throw what we had down the drain. We would only be there for three months—"So enjoy it, but don't get tied up into anything serious," we were told.

*Top: Dhoby time at St. George's Barracks in Sliema, Malta.
Bottom: The infamous Gut, Valletta, Malta.*

    I was lucky enough to be selected for the garrison football team and played against other regiments and local Maltese teams. We managed to get to the local cup final and played a semi-professional Maltese team at the stadium in Valletta. We lost 2-0 but I enjoyed every minute of it. Most of our time though was on manoeuvres further into the heart of Malta, with low flying planes mimicking some sort of attacks. We also had to learn street fighting and house clearing. This we did nearly every day for about two months. We knew it was preparing for the real thing but hoped it would never happen. The real thing of course could only be Suez Canal as Nasser was not giving in to any government who used the canal. He wanted toll money for every ship that used it, both north and south. We were hoping that either he would relent or the French and English governments would relent; if neither relented we knew we would be sent in to secure the canal for safe passage of our ships.

While we were on Malta we noticed that there were daily boat trips to Gozo, a small island off Malta. Three of us got permission from our superiors to visit Gozo and on our next day off we booked a boat trip and went to Gozo. We landed at a fishing village on the coast, had a look around the island and found there was nothing else to see. The population was all in this fishing village and they looked at us as though we were aliens. We had to wait for the boat to come back so had a cup of something in the only coffee shop on the island. The people there were so poor it was unbelievable. This was in 1956. When we boarded the boat for our return the few people watching us did not even return our farewell waving. These people were definitely in the dark ages. I believe that today the island of Gozo is a holiday resort—I wonder what the Gozo population thinks of it now? The population of it then must have been about 200 people. Gozo definitely had the potential to be a holiday resort but it was so far back in time that it would be a big undertaking to make it into a resort.

Training on Malta

*Top left: Rope crawl. Top right: Abseiling.
Botton left: Officer showing off on death slide, Malta.
Bottom right: Landing craft at Mellieha Bay, Malta*

One thing very noticeable when training on Malta for the Suez Canal invasion was the fact that the officers and N.C.O.s trained as hard and sometimes harder than ourselves.

Practising from P.L.C.s onto beach at Mellieha Bay, Malta

We knew that this training and assault landing was leading to an amphibious landing at Port Said at the northern end of the Suez Canal and we couldn't help wondering whether all of us would survive this battle.

Back to Malta and back to manoeuvres, we were now practising beach landings. We would embark on to P.L.C.s (personnel landing craft) and move around the island to Mellieha Bay. The P.L.C.s would run up onto the beach, drop their ramps and we would tumble out and run up to the nearest dunes, or any other cover there was. We did these landing manoeuvres for about two weeks, then went back to street fighting and house clearing at some deserted buildings on Malta. We had to learn to throw a grenade into a room; then, as soon as it went off, rush in and spray the room with stengun fire. We learnt that the first corner of the room to fire at was the one behind the door. It was now beginning to feel as though we were training for real.

The training was more about using your head and commonsense than brute force. We still had to be fit and had to practice until we could use a weapon naturally. We also had to practice bayonet charging just in case we got into hand-to-hand fighting. Screaming and charging at a bag of sawdust for an hour or so was okay, but what would happen if the sawdust was an Egyptian and he was charging at us? It was a bit frightening to think about, but the instructors said, "Don't worry, when the time comes, everybody rises to the occasion." I looked at him and thought, "Where do they get these instructors from? If you've got to swim you will swim, if you've got to bayonet someone, you will." How did they work this out? There was a lot of apprehension on the lads' faces, but the N.C.O.s moved us on to the next task.

It was early September when I received the letter telling me my girlfriend wanted me to come home as she was carrying my child. I requested compassionate leave and flew home. I had a weeks' leave, and we were married on the 13th September 1956 and have been married ever since. I flew back to Malta and went straight back into the training schedule. I found it was getting more serious by the day.

About the end of September we were given the weekend off. Although we were on standby, they allowed us two days of leisure. The first thing we thought of was to go to Valletta and have a good time. There was a dozen of us. We caught Garry's and hightailed it for the capital. We were in every bar down the gut and noticed quite a lot of lads from other regiments, the signals, the artillery, and there seemed to be more matelots than usual. When we enquired why, the same answer came back: it looks like we're all going to Suez.

The next day, Sunday, 'Yorky' and I hired a Garry and went into Valletta to Grand Harbour to see what ships were anchored. We knew straight away that it was for real when we saw what lay in the harbour. There were two aircraft carriers, about three destroyers, four cruisers and landing ships such as T.L.S.s (tank landing ships), T.L.C.s (tank landing crafts) and auxiliary ships. The decks were all buzzing with matelots at their tasks. We looked at each other and said, "Jesus Christ, it's for real." We caught a Garry back to the barracks to tell everyone. We were constantly on standby, which meant we were to be ready inside an hour, to move into trucks that would take us down to Valletta so we could embark onto ships ready to go. We were on standby right up until October 30th. This was when the bugle blew and onto the trucks we went. There were approximately thirty trucks full of marine commandos, all in full battle kit, wearing combat smocks, carrying ammunition and Bergen rucksacks. We were driven down to the 'MARSA' which is a quayside in Valletta harbour. We embarked onto tank landing ships and tank landing craft of the amphibious warfare squadron. The whole of 40 commando were embarked onto tank landing ships. The scene on this quayside was compared by some to the preliminaries of the Sicilian Invasion in 1943. It was really exciting but we were apprehensive as to what was going to happen next. By evening time on October 30th 1956 the Grand Harbour was empty—all ships, aircraft carriers, destroyers, cruisers, T.L.C.s and auxiliary ships were all on their way out of the harbour and heading across the Mediterranean on course for Egypt.

MALTA 37

Grand Harbour, Malta

Top: H.M.S. Theseus Aircraft Carrier
Bottom: H.M.S. Manxman mine-laying cruiser
before departure to Port Said.

St. George's Barracks, Malta

*Top: Ready, waiting for order to embark onto trucks
and move down to the 'Marsa' quayside.
Bottom: Our trucks arriving at the 'Marsa' full of commandos.*

PORT SAID

While on board we went through keep-fit drills and lectures as to our objectives daily so that it was all drilled permanently into our heads. There was a great camaraderie amongst us; both regular marines and national servicemen were as one in mind and we gained confidence from this. We non-swimmers were on a T.L.S in the middle of the Med and never worried about it. As we sailed towards Egypt other ships were joining the convoy from different parts of the Med. The French fleet was also forming the same way, from different ports. The British objective was to capture Port Said and move on down the canal to Suez at the southern end of the canal. The French objective was to capture Port Fouad and move down the east side of the canal to Suez. Port Said and Fouad are at either side of the northern end of the canal, leading into the Mediterranean. Before we did this the two battle fleets had to rendezvous about four miles off the Egyptian coast and prepare for action. Then, when we rendezvoused, came the biggest fright of our lives. We were below decks when the alarm sounded. A voice over the tannoy ordered everyone to don lifebelts and assemble on deck immediately. Apparently a submarine had come on to the sonar and all ships were at action stations.

We were all assembled on deck in orderly fashion and were then informed that the submarine had been ordered to surface or it would be depth charged. The destroyers were circling around the spot where the submarine was submerged. The destroyers were at full speed sounding their alarms as they went. We non-swimmers were visualizing floating in the water and we were a bit tensed up. The destroyers forced the submarine to surface; first the conning tower became visible, and then the sub surfaced completely. It was only about 125 yards off our port side and had an American flag printed on the conning tower. Apparently they had tracked us all the way from Malta just to make sure they knew what was going on. You could hear the sighs of relief coming from us as we saw it was an American sub. We didn't realize at the time that the Egyptians had no submarines; after all, we *were* just squaddies! The submarine was ordered not to intervene with what was going to happen and it sped away north on the surface as ordered. A destroyer went with it till it was well out of sight. The submarine had been ordered by the American government to monitor what was happening and relate back to the Americans. The next bit of excitement was the tannoy sounding again telling us that if we wanted to see the French battleship, *The Jean Barte*, we could come on deck and watch for it coming over the horizon.

It was just like a wedding cake coming over the horizon. First the top tier came in sight, then the next tier and so on until the whole ship was visible and moving towards the French fleet. The size of this battleship was unbelievable. We were on *H.M.S. Reggio* which was a tank landing ship and we felt as if we were on a tug when we realized the size of *The Jean Barte*, which must have been easily ten times the size of the *Reggio*. The battleship anchored about seven miles offshore and still looked gigantic. In the British fleet, although I can't remember all of the names, were *H.M.S. Jamaica*, *H.M.S. Ceylon*, *H.M.S. Theseus* plus other destroyers and cruisers, *T.L.S. Reggio*, plus other T.L.S.s and T.L.C.s, fleet auxiliaries, *H.M.S. Manxman*. Along with the French ships there were about 200 vessels lying off Port Said and Port Fouad by November 4th 1956.

Destination Port Said

*Top: H.M.S. 'Jamaica' and H.M.S. 'Ceylon'
—our convoy escorts to Port Said.
Bottom: H.M.T.L.S.s in convoy across the Med to Port Said.*

The cruisers of both fleets lined up broadside about four miles out to sea ready for the naval bombardment. The *Jean Barte* was broadside about seven miles out at sea; it was going to fire its guns over the top of the cruisers. This lining up of cruisers and battleship was amazing to watch. The destroyers were racing around on alert behind the cruisers ready to protect the T.L.S.s and T.L.C.s from attack. We knew it was close to 'H' hour but were still watching the big ships readying themselves. Another good point for us was the fact that the aircraft carriers were way beyond the horizon and we were waiting to see the planes fly over for the aerial bombardment. Also, there were the the para's to be dropped onto the airfield on the west side of Port Said; it was their job to capture the airfield so we could fly troops and gear in and use the airfield for our convenience.

PORT SAID   43

On board H.M.T.L.C. 'Reggio' on route to Port Said

Top: Cleaning weapons and priming grenades ready for assault.
Bottom: In we go, P.L.C.s heading for beach and Port Said.
H.M.S. 'Jamaica' in right-hand corner.

AMPHIBIOUS LANDING

This was certainly some adventure. Although we were all a bit nervous, you could not be more impressed than watching all this ship manoeuvring happening. Just then, the tannoy called: "All marines report to lower deck." We were already kitted up ready to go so knew this was it—the 'H' hour. We were formed up below ready to listen to our colonel-in-chief brief us. After this briefing the colonel said that one bit of good news was the fact that we would land on the beaches wearing our green berets and not wearing helmets. We used to dread wearing helmets, so we cheered him. His last words were, "Good luck, marines, and I'll see you all soon." He left the troop captains and other officers to brief us on our troop objectives. I was in 'A' troop and our objective was a block of flats, the first building in Port Said from the beach. I thought it was a hotel but it was a block of flats. We had to capture this and secure it, then move to our next objective. When the briefing was over we were ordered to assemble on deck ready to move into assault craft. We went up on deck and realized that the invasion had started. There were jets flying in firing rockets and machine guns at a row of beach huts about 30 yards up the beach, some of which were already ablaze. We looked at that (four miles away) and thought, 'Jesus, we have to get through that to see our first objective!' We were standing waiting for the signal to board the assault craft when there was such an almighty noise. It was a broadside from the cruisers; the first shots were fired, the whistle went and over we had to go, down the scramble net and into the assault craft. The assault crafts had been lowered from the T.L.S. as we were being briefed. Again there was another almighty noise as the cruisers fired another broadside. Our bottoms were starting to twitch a bit.

Cruiser bombardment

Top: Port Said straight ahead.
Bottom: 'A' Troop's first objective was to get beyond the burning beach huts and locate the block of flats we had to secure.

When we were all into the assault craft we moved away from the *Reggio* and began circling until every single assault craft was loaded with marines. Again the cruisers fired their broadside. When all the assault craft were ready, the flare went up and signalled the moment to form up and do the amphibious landing. In the meantime, para's had been dropped onto the airfield. The jets were still diving and firing rockets and machine guns into Port Said and the same was happening with the French at Port Fouad. The legionnaires had dropped into Port Fouad by parachute and had met heavy resistance; this was on the wireless the royal signaller had who was attached to our troop. In all of our landing crafts were 40 commando and 42 commando. The whole of the beach on the Port Said side had to be secured by these marines. It was 4.45 a.m. on November 6th 1956 and we were on our way. When all of the assault craft got the 'go' signal they had to move into full speed (depending on the state of the sea), head for the gaps in-between the cruisers and go for the beach—bearing in mind they all had to hit the beach simultaneously.

We were scared, to say the least, but the next thing that happened almost made us mess our pants! As we were passing in-between the cruisers, they broadsided and the noise nearly blew our eardrums out. It was unbelievable stuff. As they fired these broadsides the recoil of their huge guns lifted the cruisers about ten metres back. What a fright! I looked at Jimmy Shade and he looked at me—we were both as white as sheets. Is this real or is it a nightmare? Still, the assault crafts kept on going. We could see just over the craft's side and saw the beach huts that were all now on fire, some even exploding.

Burning beach huts

'A' Troop's task was to get through these beach huts and get down just beyond them.
The block of flats about 100 yards beyond the burning huts had to be taken and secured. The next task was to secure Consul House and then move on to meet up with the 42 Commando at the Garden Square in the centre of Port Said.

The gyppos had apparently filled a few of them with explosives. While all of this was going on the jets were still straffing the beach and everything beyond that. The whole town seemed to be burning. We then heard that the para's had control of the airfield—there was still some resistance but it was nearly secure. Our job was next. Two words spoken by the officer in charge to the sergeant nearly had us messing our pants again. "Fix bayonets!" shouted the sergeant. I'm sure you could have heard him above all the noise the cruisers were making. Bayonets fixed, we looked at one another and then never looked at each other again until the day was over. Then there was a thud as the amphibious craft hit the beach and ran up the sand about 10 or 15 metres. The assault craft had a matelot as the driver (for want of a better word) and he had to press the switch to let the ramp down so we could run out and do our job. Guess what? The switch didn't work, which meant we were sitting ducks for a grenade or shell landing in the craft. Three times he pressed it, three times nothing happened. "Somebody kick it down!" shouted the matelot. To do that someone had to get on top, in full view of any gyppo, and kick it from the top. For a split second everyone was paralysed, then up jumped the big Cockney and in full view of the enemy he kicked at it twice. The second time it released. We all poured out to what was in store for us.

Next time I saw the Cockney I told him he deserved a medal as big as a frying pan for what he had done. We would still have been in the assault craft if he hadn't jumped up and kicked the ramp down. When we came out of the craft we made for the beach huts. Luckily there was enough room under them to scamper through to the dune behind them and the odd gap between them.

"Down!" came the order. We were down before the N.C.O. finished saying it. There was some sniping fire coming from the block of flats, about 100 yards away. To get to our objective we had to cross a grassed area with about a half dozen shrubs at random in-between us and the flats. There were some Egyptians to the right of the flats but they were leaving their anti-tank guns and running back to Port Said. The order was to shoot them and this we did, albeit, probably in their backs. Then the sniping from the flats increased—from one window someone was firing a machine gun. Tony Davies fixed an energa bomb to his rifle and fired it straight into the window where the machine gun was. The bomb exploded and blew the whole window out. There was no more firing from that room. I was still asking myself "Is this real?" when the order came to advance across this 100-yard lawn at the double. I did it at the treble. Halfway across, due to sniping fire, the order came to down and take cover. I immediately jumped behind one of the shrubs. The shrubs were about 6 feet high and about 4 feet wide. To my surprise, another five or six squaddies had the same idea. Some of us were lying on top of one another; I guess this happened at the other shrubs as well. I swear that none of us could be seen. In training we would be saying to each other "Get away and find your own shrub!" but this was different, this was for real. When the next order came I noticed briefly that the jets had stopped straffing and the naval bombardment had ceased. The next order that came was to get to the block of flats as fast as possible. This we did but on the way we were shot at by snipers in the building. The distance to cover was about fifty yards. On the way the bren gun ammunition carrier's pouch straps either snapped or became loose, for he was now running towards the objective with ammunition pouches sliding down his body with every pace he took. I shouted for him to keep going but he was clearly panicking; he eventually got to the flats with the pouches around his ankles. He was a good lad and showed his relief at reaching the outside of the flats. The sergeant told him 'well done' and we felt better. A couple of the marines were wounded but nothing serious.

'A' Troop's First Objective

Top: 'A' Troop's next objective was Consul House, behind these flats. Bottom: This was taken after ceasefire was called. Tony Davie's energa bomb caused the damage to the third floor window.

PORT SAID SECURE

When we were all pressed hard up against the outside of the flats, the sergeant gave us our orders. There were seven storeys of flats and each flat and room had to be secured. Judging by the sniping fire it was estimated that there would probably be fifteen to twenty of the enemy still in these flats. The flats had to be cleared floor by floor. This meant opening the door, throwing in the grenade, running straight in after the grenade exploded and shooting anyone who was still alive in there. Before we entered through the main door we were ordered not to shoot civilians. Little did we know that the Egyptian soldiers had guessed this and when they knew they were not going to win this battle, they changed into civvies and pleaded innocence. This apparently was happening all over Port Said. I suppose it was happening in Port Fouad as well. Anyhow, we still had to secure this building so in went the grenades into the foyer. Straight after the grenades went off, we went in. We ran to any door that was still closed, some to the foot of the stairs and some to the rear entrance. The lift was on its way down; the bren gun was positioned to fire at the lift. When it stopped at ground level the doors opened and two civilians stepped out with their hands in the air. These were quickly ushered away as prisoners. The lift was put out of commission so that no one else could use it; whether those two civilians were soldiers in civilian clothes we were not to know. And how on earth we hadn't shot them as they came out of the lift I'll never know. We were all becoming trigger-happy and self-preservation was very obvious. These two Egyptians had been extremely lucky.

'A' TROOPS OBJECTIVES

The job now was to clear the stairway and disperse about a dozen marines to each floor. A second lieutenant and a sergeant and corporal were in charge of our squad. We started along the corridor; grenades into the rooms, in with stenguns—the first two flats on our floor were empty. The next flat was the one where the energa bomb had blown the window out. There were two dead Egyptians and one wounded, moaning. The bomb had wrecked the room, the machine gun was decimated—the bomb had been spot on. We found some rifles, ammunition and grenades in one room and it looked as though these had been left and the personnel had scarpered. We thought about the two civilians, but had to stay focused. A little bit relaxed, we made our way to the remaining flat. Tragedy was about to happen. The officer shot the lock off the door with his stengun and the sergeant threw the grenade in. It went off. In ran the officer and pointed his stengun at the corner behind the door. Two Arabs were sitting slightly stunned by the explosion. The officer in self-preservation pulled the trigger, but nothing happened—the stengun had jammed! The two Arabs, again in self-preservation, opened fire and shot the officer dead. The sergeant was in like a raging bull. He shot the Arabs to death and would have still been firing if the corporal hadn't calmed him down. We had lost an officer just through a stengun jamming! All of this happened in the space of about five or six seconds. We were now right on the edge. When the flats were secured we had about a dozen prisoners and a sizeable haul of weapons. The prisoners were all in civilian clothes and had apparently surrendered. Captain Grant was in one hell of a mood, having just lost an officer; he would have shot the prisoners but thought about it and handed them over to the people who were to take control of all prisoners. We regrouped and set about our next objective, which was the consul house. In the other parts of Port Said, the para's had total control of the airfield, 42 commando and 45 commando had advanced into the heart of the port, and the French had made hard work of taking Port Fouad and had by all accounts met really stiff opposition. They had lost a lot of men (foreign legion, I believe) but had secured the port.

Port Said
Disembarking

Top: Centurion tanks coming ashore. Ready to move down the canal to Suez.
Bottom: Royal Marine Commandos securing the Port of Port Said.

While regrouping I noticed that where we had landed was covered with tanks, trucks, jeeps, big guns, and the infantry were disembarking. The ammunition was coming ashore in tons. The lawn that we had run across was all churned up with the beachhead traffic. It was reassuring to us all, seeing this happening. It was still hard to take in what was happening. The British certainly knew how to go to war. Before we moved to our next objective we had to find out where the shells were coming from; they were whistling up the main road up our side of the canal and exploding just short of the flats. I was in a patrol led by Captain Grant who was, to my mind, enjoying every moment of this battle. He was still fuming about the officer who was killed and seemed intent on revenge. There were about six of us riflemen and a corporal.

Tragedy was again about to happen. We were sniped at as we crossed the road and as we ran across in line we would be a hard target, but no one was hurt. We reached this circular stone building similar to a Martello. It was obviously a canal office that must have been used to take the particulars of any ship or boat that entered the canal. This seemed to be the British command post. As we came to it we saw that an anti-tank gun was being assembled on the flat roof of this building. The building had a fort like parapet around the roof, about two feet high. The anti-tank gun and crew were attached to the commando units. The gun that was firing at us had been located and our gun was being put together to silence it. We were all lying in different places behind the building; the signaller attached to us was sitting, with his wireless, behind the command post and talking to the captain when the gun fired. The back blast of the gun must have loosened the parapet; the gun fired again and blew the parapet (with its back blast) onto the signaller's head. When the commotion which had broken out calmed down, the signaller looked dead. The medics got to him as fast as they could; we dragged the stones off him and noticed a thin blue line down his face to his jaw. This, according to the medics, meant he had fractured his whole head. He was whipped away still alive. Whether he survived or not we never found out. We do know that the anti-tank gun knocked out the gun that was tying us down. When you hear about friendly fire, this one has to take the biscuit. I sincerely hope the signaller survived.

As we went back to the flats we were sniped at from the British consul, which was our next objective. We had to secure this objective and meet up with 42 commando at the square in the middle of Port Said. As we made our way we couldn't help but notice the scuttled ships in the canal. They had been scuttled to lie across the canal to stop ships using the canal. We also noticed the trucks, guns, tanks, jeeps and infantrymen that had amassed at the mouth of the canal. The same had happened on the other side at Port Fouad. The allies really meant business. It was only 8 a.m. and the amount of material and men that were disembarked was phenomenal.

As we stealthily approached the consul we noticed about a dozen civilians walking away from the entrance. We had them covered ready to fire when we were ordered to let them go. The entrance to the consul was about 75 yards away and we could have shot them all but they were in civilian clothes so even though we knew they would be soldiers, we obeyed orders. The sniping had stopped and when we went into the building and went from room to room we found it empty. There were a lot of guns of various makes and I thought no wonder they were poor shots. One room was full of ammunition of all descriptions. When this building was secure we had to regroup and make our way to the square in Port Said.

JARDINIERRE SQUARE

As we made our way to the square we were escorted by our amphibian personnel carriers and centurion tanks. There was very little resistance, just the odd sniper and these were taken out by the tanks' guns. They were pinpointed and their positions were given to the tank commander who saw to it that they were blown to kingdom come. We now felt very secure. We saw plenty of bodies lying around, mostly in uniform but civilians were still surrendering. Were these soldiers who had donned civvies and pleaded innocence? We couldn't tell. They were rounded up and escorted to a compound. All in all there was very little damage to the buildings, except where snipers had been taken out. It seemed to me that the jets and cruisers had hit nearly all the military targets and had caused very little damage to civilian buildings. Earlier, 45 commando had been flown in by helicopter from *H.M.S. Ocean*, an aircraft carrier, and had secured all their objectives. Forty-two commando had finally secured theirs and we in 40 commando just had to reach the square and we would have done our job. It was around noon when we reached the square and engaged in a shooting match with some diehards. This didn't last very long—there was practically no cover in the square and they became sitting ducks. Some were killed and the rest surrendered. We then took up our positions down one side of the square. It was a huge square called, I think, 'Jardinierre Square'.

The square was approximately 200 yards by 200 yards with a few bushes and palm trees in it. We counted fourteen dead Egyptian soldiers lying in different spots. The sun was high in the sky and it was very hot. We got ourselves under the cover of the canopy along the main road next to the square to keep out of the sun, positioned behind the pillars that were approximately 12 feet apart. We then heard that they were trying to negotiate a ceasefire. This was good news since we did not want to lose anyone else.

Just then, further along the street, a man came out of the post office and proceeded to walk away from us. Our corporal shouted at him to stop but he just kept on going. He shouted again but he still did not stop. The corporal then lifted his rifle and fired at him. The man fell but was still alive. When we got to him he had propped himself against the wall and he was just sitting there. The bullet had torn half of his face away and his face was covered with flies at his blood. What a ghastly sight. When asked why he had shot the man the corporal replied that he thought he was a looter. The officer accepted this and the man was taken away by our medics. Whether he was a looter never came to light. But again, self-preservation came to the fore and we soon forgot about it. We were then informed that all hostilities had ceased—a ceasefire had been called.

CEASEFIRE

The generals and officers were not happy about the ceasefire as they knew the canal was there for the taking. It would probably have taken less than a week to move down the canal to Suez, and the generals said this to our government but were told to stay put in Port Said and get the port back to normal. The French were in the same dilemma—they did not like this situation either, as they had lost a lot of men and had begun to move down the east side of the canal towards Suez. Both the French and our lot were roughly about two or three miles out of Fouad and Port Said moving towards Suez when the order to stop was issued. It was about 5 p.m. when the ceasefire came. It was just turning dark so we had to settle in where we were till morning. We found out the next morning that the Americans had put pressure on the French and British governments to cease hostilities and negotiate with the Egyptians and President Nasser. This was to cost Prime Minister Anthony Eden his job—he resigned shortly after the Suez crisis. I was still in my position the next morning when the mail arrived. The marine who gave the mail out said, "Here, Geordie, there's a nice letter for you." It was about 8 a.m. and it was really hot when I looked at this envelope. It was a letter from the Inland Revenue wanting to know my status and earnings since my marriage! I was not pleased about this. Here I was in Port Said, in the Suez crisis, risking life and limb for my country, and the taxman was after me! Everyone just laughed but I can tell you I was *not* pleased. I couldn't stop thinking about it all day.

The Square—Every little helps

Top left: This Square was 'A' Troop's last objective.
Top right: This was our undercover agent in Port Said!
Bottom left: 'Geordie Cox' with captured weapons.
Bottom right: Weapon cleaning after ceasefire.

When the ceasefire was duly implemented, the Egyptian civilians started about their usual business as though nothing had happened. Whether they were soldiers in civvies, we couldn't tell.

At about 2 p.m. we were given orders to requisition dwellings that were empty and set up billeting in them. We chose a dwelling overlooking the square. It had three floors and was very comfortable. It belonged to an Egyptian police commander and he and his family had moved out just before the invasion took place. We were in this house for about three or four days when the order came telling us we had to leave Port Said by troopship back to Malta. 40 and 45 commandos had to leave on the *Empire Fowey* troopship and 42 commando had to stay in the port for a little while longer.

Return to Malta

Top left: Waiting to embark at Port Said onto Troopship 'Empire Fowey'.
Top right: Relaxing on board Troopship 'Empire Fowey' on route to Malta.
Bottom: H.M. Troopship 'Empire Fowey' at anchor back in Grand Harbour, Malta.

Two or three days later we were marched back to the port's quayside and embarked on to the *Empire Fowey* troopship. It was some size! When all of the troops were on board, the ship cast off and made its way into the Med, heading for Malta. On our way back to Malta we talked about the things that had happened and were really relieved that we had survived and we said we would get rotten drunk when we reached Malta.

On Saturday 17th November 1956 we sailed into Grand Harbour to be greeted by hundreds of people cheering and clapping us home. We had to realize that nearly all of the regular marines plus officers were in married quarters on Malta and it was these relations who had turned up to cheer us in. We national servicemen enjoyed this as well; it was good to see Captain Grant being hugged by his wife and the N.C.O.s embracing their wives and children. As for us, we just wanted to get to barracks in Sliema, get cleaned up and get down to Valetta as quick as possible. What a night we had that night! It was a great relief to be at ease and enjoying ourselves again.

The next three months were spent on Malta in St. Georges barracks, and after Suez everything seemed very boring, even though we still did some sort of manoeuvres and guards. I played a lot of football for the garrison, which I was happy about. We also visited every part of Malta and admired their churches and historic buildings, but we always looked forward to a night out in Valletta, down the infamous gut. We also visited Comino, another small island off Malta. There was nothing there, just a few very poor inhabitants. We also visited Paola, Birkirkara, Rabat and Mosta, all on Malta. The Maltese were very nice people and always welcoming.

'Pine Tree Camp', Cyprus

Top: Troodos
Centre: Author about to throw a snowball.
Bottom: Author and Jimmy Shade.

RETURN TO CYPRUS

We were beginning to think there was nothing exciting going to happen in our second year of national service when word started going around that 40 commando were to be on the move again around the middle of February 1957. At last the order came and to our surprise, the destination was put up on the orders board—it was to be Cyprus again. This tour of duty was to take us up to the highest point in Cyprus, Mount Olympus. We had to take over from the parachute regiment, based at this camp very near the top of Mount Olympus in the Troodos mountain range. The mountains were capped with snow and it was very cold at nights. About a mile down the mountain the weather was a great deal warmer with no snow at all. The name of the camp was 'Pine Tree Camp', quite appropriate as the mountain slopes were covered with pine trees. There was a village about one and a half miles down the mountain called Amiandos; the inhabitants made their living there by quarrying asbestos. We were called out a couple of times to Amiandos as they were noted for feeding terrorists, but we never caught them out.

On a clear day you could see across the island to the north, to the town of Kyrenia, and on a really good day, Greece and Turkey were clearly visible. This was from the top of Olympus, of course. Doing our national service certainly allowed us to be at places we couldn't even imagine in Civvy Street. Our duties on this tour of duty were more or less the same as before—helping at police stations and going on search patrols. When we were off duty we could visit Niscosia, in groups of course, taken in trucks. Kyrenia as well. Limassol was our favourite; there were British forces in these towns—the RAF in Limassol and other regiments in the other towns. Out of bounds in all these simply meant this and were patrolled by military police. Getting caught in the out of bounds area meant being on a charge, for security reasons.

Skiing on Mount Olympus, Cyprus

Top: Slipping away
Centre: Troodos—view from road up to Mt. Olympus.
Bottom: Paddy Armstrong, Terry Jones, 'Slim' Wooden.

Sometimes when we were off duty we were allowed out of the camp to go skiing. We weren't very good at it but we always had a laugh. When it was our turn for police station duty we were taken by truck to a village named Pano Panayia, the village where Makarias was born. There was very little there and the people were very poor. It was the same routine as before, one policeman and one marine on watch while the others slept or played cards listening to the radio. Nothing ever happened when we were there and we were glad to get back to 'Pine Tree'.

One night we were called out to a village where there was supposed to be a terrorist coming in for food and ammunition. We surrounded the village at the dead of night, around midnight. It was pitch black; the only thing visible was candlelight coming from the holes in the shuttered windows. Everything was still, when suddenly we heard a noise. We tensed up as the noise came closer. Just then a door opened at this hovel of a house just about 50 yards away and a man emerged. We thought, 'This is it!' Remaining still and perfectly hidden, the noise got closer until we realized it was a donkey. The man from the house stopped about 30 yards from his door, dropped his pantaloons, did his business and then went back into the house. We couldn't speak, couldn't even laugh for fear of giving our positions away. Nothing else happened that night and we boarded the trucks the next morning laughing our socks off. We had been alerted by a donkey and a bloke that had a crap just 20 yards away from our position. So much for the terrorists! The officer and N.C.O.s enjoyed the laugh as well.

68   Royal Marines 1955–1957

Terrorist in disguise

Top: 'Silly Ass'
Bottom: Myself and 'Tich' Bradley with locals at their coffee shop.

These people are Turkish Cypriots and are very poor—as you can see—but were very friendly and obviously glad that the British forces were there to protect them.

The next time we went out on police duty it was to a village called Alona. There was Sergeant Potter, Corporal Bellas and six marines. We met the three policemen (Turkish Cypriots), whose names were Memeht, Bahi and Nevsat. It was hard to tell who was in charge of the policemen but we settled for Nevsat. After organizing the watches Sgt. Potter tried to organize the policemen into who was on watch first with me. They were very uptight as they'd had experience with terrorists and they made it clear their lives were under threat. The one selected for midnight watch with me was Memeht. We went to the observation post and he immediately started singing; apparently he was singing loudly to let the terrorists (if any were about) know that the police station was manned. He thought that if he sang loud enough the terrorists would not come this way. It was pitch black and here I was on guard with a Turkish policeman singing "*ish ki dara gud da arikin ul dal a bidi mur*" all night long. We just couldn't shut him up. I was now as frightened as he was. In the morning, Nevsat explained that Memeht was as frightened as a kitten each time he was on police station duty—he would sing all night no matter who was on guard with him. Seeing as no one wanted to be a policeman they had to put up with him. Honestly, he was like a scared rabbit every time he had to do police station duty! He preferred being in the village police station, not the stations outside of the village. We were glad when we were relieved from duty at the Alona police station outpost. When off duty we used to go into the village and have a cup of coffee or soft drinks with the locals. The locals all said that Memeht was too frightened to be a policeman but nobody else would have the job because terrorists always went for policemen first if the attacked a village.

'Alona' Police Station

Top: Sgt. Potter. 'Tich' Bradley, myself, 'Slim' Wooden, A.N. Other, 'Geordie' Cox, Cpl. Bellas, 'Ginger' Hoar, at 'Alona' police Station.
Bottom left: 'Tich' Bradley, myself and Nevsat,
Bottom right: Memeht, Cpl. Bellas, Bahi, Nevsat, myself.

The policemen were Turkish Cypriots and very friendly. Although they were frightened, they stuck at it and were glad when the term at the police outpost was over.

After two or three days in camp there was an alert. Half of the camp were called to embark onto trucks and proceed to a certain place in the forest. We could see from the camp as we embarked that there was a forest fire about ten miles away, around a river. The fire had been started by terrorists (supposedly) and had trapped some British soldiers who were, in fact, searching for terrorists. We disembarked from the trucks (about 100 of us) near to where the fire had started. We had to follow the forest paths down to the stream and follow the stream through the burnt-out trees and undergrowth, always being wary of any terrorists lurking. When we reached the command post we observed medics everywhere. There were a lot of bodies, all burnt beyond recognition (about 12 bodies). The colonel was in a bit of a state, understandably so—the loss of these soldiers in this manner was hard to accept. The medics were tending to other soldiers who were also burnt, but alive, and someone else was taking the nametags off the dead and covering them over. It was a terrible sight and one or two of our lads were really sick. Our leader was given the estimated positions of the terrorists and we were immediately dispatched in patrols to see if we could locate them. The soldiers who were caught in the fire were from a Welsh regiment, I think. We did not know this for sure but when they spoke it seemed to be a Welsh accent.

As we passed the rest of the soldiers, who were sitting along the tracks, we saw that they were in a very emotional state, having been caught like this. They were shouting, "Get the bastards!" So we set off, determined to avenge these lads. Apparently General George Grivas had been seen with these terrorists and this unit of soldiers had been dispatched hurriedly to the scene and had been trapped in this forest fire. We searched and searched in the area the terrorists were supposed to be. We searched until it was too dark and bivouacked till dawn the next day. It looked as though they had slipped away from us, until we came across this valley. It was a huge clearing, treeless, and the valley floor was all stones. Right at the bottom of this valley was a beautiful church. "They must be in there," whispered our captain. The church was about 200 yards away and right in the middle of this stony valley. If they were in there we would be able to see them if they made a break for it.

When all of the patrols came together the plan was to send some marines down each side and when they were in position for the three groups to advance on foot towards the church. This meant it was like a pincer movement with three sides covered. This we did and as no one came out of the church to try to flee back into the forest on the open side, we expected a free-for-all gunfight. This didn't happen and when we got to the church we were all on edge as to what was going to happen next. Nothing happened. The doors were opened, but there was not a soul in there—although there was evidence of them having been there. They were gone and we never came into contact with them. We stayed for about two hours before we made tracks back to our rendezvous to be picked up by lorries. In the two hours we went into the church and had a good look at the architecture and the statues. We marvelled at the design and priceless things that were in there. Why it had been built in that stony valley was anybody's guess, for there wasn't a village for miles. We were under orders not to touch or remove anything. I couldn't be certain, but I thought it was a Greek church. Anyhow, we made our way to the rendezvous, boarded the trucks and headed back to Pine Tree Camp.

FATEFUL AMBUSH

The next two or three weeks were spent on police station duty, patrolling the forest area, doing camp guard duty and a couple of times visiting Niscosia, Kyrenia or Limassol. It was looking as though this was going to be all we could do until one night at about 2 a.m. The camp was alerted, ordered to get ready with weapons and live ammunition and board the trucks that were waiting for us, engines running and ready to go. Earlier a patrol had been sent out to a village named Pelendria where terrorists were expected to come in for food, etc. The patrol had set up an ambush down the track that came into the village. The patrol consisted of the usual: marines, sergeant, corporal and lieutenant Haynes. They had set this ambush up with the bren guns facing down the track and marines either side facing the same way. If anyone came up the track towards the village they had to be stopped. It was pitch black and hard to see so they had to listen intently.

After hearing the noise of someone coming up the track the officer in charge had to shout, "Halt, Stamata, Durr!"—which was the English, Greek and Turkish words for 'Stop.' He did this and apparently as he said these orders he stood up (which is something you shouldn't do when you've set an ambush). The leading terrorist, bearing in mind that it was too dark to see anyone, opened fire with a light machine gun and sprayed bullets in an arc across the ambush area. He did this and killed Lieutenant Haynes instantly. Immediately afterwards the bren gun plus the marines opened fire in retaliation. The leading terrorist was killed and two others were wounded. The wounded terrorists escaped back into the forest, leaving a trail of blood, not seen until daylight.

At first light (about 4 a.m.) we arrived in trucks. Some marines were dispatched to surround the village and some were ordered to turn all of the villagers out of their homes and herd them on to a piece of flat waste land just on the outskirts of the village for interrogation. We were shown where the ambush had taken place, and the body of the terrorist was still lying there. Lieutenant Haynes was body-bagged and taken to camp. In the village coffee shop there were about a half dozen men. We were ordered to get them out and place them with the other villagers; this we did with exception of the eldest one who refused to move. We were trying to coax him out as he was about 60 years old, when an officer walked in, pushed us out of the way and hit the man with the butt of his stengun. The man collapsed, unconscious. We were aghast at this; the officer looked at us and said, "Carry him out and put him with the rest of the villagers." We did as we were ordered.

All of the officers and N.C.O's were in a foul mood at the thought of losing an officer in a dead end place like this, especially one who was as well liked as Lt. Haynes. When every one of the villagers was in the interrogation area, the houses and huts, etc., were all searched and left in disarray. The sun was up and it was becoming very warm; we were all lathered with sweat and, probably, in trepidation of what was going to happen next.

What happened next was unbelievable! The officers and N.C.O.s (who were still fuming over our loss of an officer) brought a jeep to where the dead terrorist was lying, tied him to the back of the jeep and dragged him through the village, past the villagers so they could see him. This terrorist had about 15 or 20 bullet holes in him so we couldn't see the point of this. If anything, it probably made the villagers hate us all the more. We national servicemen thought that since the man had been identified as a terrorist from the photographs which were produced and we had got him, why lower ourselves to this level? It was probably the stigma and frustration of losing one of our own. Still, we had to obey orders so we just did what we were instructed. An army unit arrived with interpreters to do the interrogation so we handed the job over to them and boarded the trucks to return to camp. The conversation in the trucks was about what had taken place. It seemed so unreal, but we had taken part in it and had to forget it and move on.

Top left: 'Pelendria' village. Lt. Haynes lost his life here.
Top right: The whole village was turned out for interrogation.
Centre: These two photographs were taken at a village named 'Kissonerga' and are used to illustrate what happened.
Bottom: 'Shags' Moorcroft, S.I.B. Interrogator, 'Rog' Davis on the path into the village. Ambush was here.

We kind of felt that eventually the Greeks would take this island and push the Turks off it.

The Turks invaded in 1974 and took the eastern end, leaving the Greek Cypriots the other two-thirds of the island (Troodos and the whole of the South West) including Paphos, Limassol, Larnaca, Nicosia and all the villages in this area. The Turkish Cypriots now occupy the tail at the eastern end of the island and the towns of Kyrenia and Famagusta, and all the villages in that area, about one third of the island. So, in hindsight, what were we doing there? Why did all these lads who lost their lives on Cyprus have to die for a lost cause? The only thing that came to my mind that had to be the answer was 'strategy'—we had to have staging places in the Middle East and, just like Malta, Cyprus was ideal. Cyprus is a beautiful island now, enjoying tourism, and I hope the villages of Ktima, Kissonerga, Polis, Stroumbi, Pano Panayia, Kyperounda, Lefka, Emba, Myrtou, Alona, Morphou, Pelendria, Amiandos and their inhabitants are living a better life as a result of this.

RETURN TO MALTA

We now had about three weeks left of our tour of duty on the island. This time was taken up with the same routine, patrols, police station duties and the occasional off duty trips into Niscosia. We would be relieved by a British regiment and transported by ship to Malta. I used to look forward to these moves by ship as you could sleep on deck as the Med was always like a millpond.

We arrived at Grand Harbour and were taken by truck up to Sliema and St. Georges barracks where we quickly settled in. After approximately two weeks we were on the move again. This time we were to be on manoeuvres at different places around the Mediterranean. We national service lads had about nine weeks to demobilization and we were looking forward to that date. However, when we heard we were going to North Africa, we sort of looked forward to this as well. Our next tour of duty after North Africa was to be Sardinia and after that we would be allowed one day's leave in Naples. That was the beauty with the marines—they were always on the move, never staying on the same tour of duty for long. I enjoyed it. Although there were times when we were scared out of our wits, it was exciting.

Top: Cup Final in Valletta. Author underlined.
Bottom: St. George's Barracks. 'Mick' Gurton, myself, Tony Davies, 'Rog' Davis, A.N. Other approximately 9 weeks before demobilisation. With Operation 'STAYSAIL' to come and a 2 or 3 day manoeuvre on Sardinia followed by a day's leave in Naples, then home and demob. It's a grand life in the Marines and how we all had enjoyed it—never a dull moment!

Operation 'Staysail'

The exercise in North Africa was named 'Staysail.' There was to be a rehearsal near Benghazi with 'A' troop and 'Y' troop of 40 commando going ashore in assault landing craft from *H.M.T.L.C. Reggio*. The other ships involved were *H.M.T.L.C. Striker*, *H.M.T.L.C. Bastion*, *H.M.T.L.C Redoubt* and *H.M.M.L. 2583*. It was very dark and we had to get out of the landing craft fast and head inland to some cover, get down and prepare to defend the beachhead. No one knew we were there except some dogs that were barking right up till dawn. When we looked around there was a village built with stone and corrugated iron sheets—hovels. To our rear we were amazed at what had been done during the night; there were trucks, jeeps, guns and ammunition ashore—amazing. This feat of engineering then had to be all loaded back onto the ships and taken about 40 miles east along the coastline to a place called Sidi Abdul ElGader where exercise 'Staysail' would take place. We reached this place in daylight and had to wait until dark before 'Staysail' began.

'A' troop had to go in first and establish a perimeter while the beachhead was set up. The second wave of craft came in, with the 'Y' troop to move west of the beachhead and dig in to defend against enemy coming from that direction. 'A' troop then had to send out two patrols, one to go east and to rendezvous with 'Partisans.' I was in the second patrol that had to trek into some low hills to the south, and bring back a 'Partisan' leader.

'H' hour was about 11 p.m. and we had to be back before dawn to re-embark and make our getaway. Every so often we met an umpire who was making notes on how we were doing. We could see flares and hear shooting to our left about 200 yards away. We kept on going to our rendezvous and reached it on time. It was still very dark when we found this so-called partisan leader, identified him as the objective and escorted him back to the beachhead.

RETURN TO MALTA 81

Top left: H.M.T.L.C.s crossing the Med on 'Staysail'.
Top right: 'Geordie' Kell, 'Geordie' Cox, 'Geordie' Lofthouse.
Centre left: 5 'Geordie' Marines.
Centre right: Heading inland.
Bottom: 'Staysail' was a training operation played out somewhere near Benghazi, North Africa. This was to be followed by manoeuvres on Sardinia, then leave in Naples.

When we arrived at the beachhead we rested and Jock Miller said he thought he recognized the partisan's voice. We told him to stop being daft! He had a blanket over his head when we reported to our chiefs. When he had been identified as the man we had went for, he came over to our troop, who were sitting in a group, and said, "Well done, 'A' troop, don't you know who I am?" It then dawned on us that not all of 'A' troop knew him; he was national service and had recognized a few of us national servicemen who had been recruited with him. It was Russell Poulding, one of the batch that joined up with myself and a few others in 'A' troop. We had to call him 'Sir,' but he shook our hands and said he was glad to see us again. He was now a lieutenant. I think I have spelt his surname correctly—if not, it must be 'Polden'. His father definitely compiled the Royal Marine manuals, so his surname will be in the manuals somewhere. It was strange that we had come across Russell like this because we hadn't seen him since he had been one of the two lads taken out of the squad to become an officer, nearly two years previously.

'Exercise Staysail' came to an end and we were on board the *Reggio* and heading for Sardinia. This was another exercise, to try out new or different landing craft. We were really looking forward to being on Sardinia albeit by landing craft, because we knew that at the end of these landing craft trials we would be heading off to Italy and a day's shore leave in Naples. When the powers that be were satisfied that the landing craft would be okay and that we could handle these craft okay, we embarked on the *Reggio* and set sail for Italy and Naples. We had been allowed to visit a town in Sardinia but we weren't excited about this as all of the people we had met while doing the training landings were very poor—nice folk, but poor. The town we visited wasn't that much better than a Cypriot village. The island itself was beautiful but barren of population for miles. Beautiful beaches surround the island but the locals, if you could find any, weren't interested.

In the town there were some motorcars but most people walked or rode on Donkeys. I suppose the island is more up-to-date now.

Top: El Adem, North Africa.
Centre: Exercises on Sardinia Island.
Bottom: H.M.T.L.C. 'Reggio' anchored off Sardinia.
After the manoeuvres we were allowed to splash about!

NAPOLI

"Naples, here we come!" was the cry from all aboard the *Reggio*. When we sailed into Naples harbour we observed the volcano Vesuvius to the south east of Naples was smoking. One marine shouted out, "God's sakes men, we're lathered, don't say we're going to get lavared as well!" We all had a good laugh at this. When we anchored, we were called below decks and briefed as to what was all right and what was not all right when we went ashore. Some parts of Naples were no-go areas and if caught in these areas one would be on a charge. Needless to say we practically all were intent on visiting these no-go areas.

Dressed in our dress denims we were ready for anything. We boarded motor launches and into Naples we went. The city itself was beautiful. Three of us had a good look around at forts, fountains, cafes (where the coffee was fantastic) and every historical building in Naples. The no-go areas were always at the back of our minds, however. We were down back streets, alleys and other roads but couldn't seem to find a 'no-go' area. We were just about to have a meal and coffee at this coffee shop when a local said something to us; we couldn't quite understand what he was saying but we used our hands and fingers to indicate what we were looking for. He pointed along the main drag at some posh buildings. We looked and thought 'he doesn't know what we mean,' but he insisted so we gave him some lira and headed off into the area he had designated.

When we came to the first door it opened and a satisfied Italian emerged. 'This is it,' we thought. We knocked on the door and pushed it open. Sitting just inside the door was a big fat Madame and just behind her was a turnstile. Apparently you had to pay the Madame and go through the turnstile and up the stairs, where it was all supposed to happen. They were brothels all right, but run by the state or the council. The Madame shouted through to another room and a man built like Goliath appeared. She looked at us and said, inquisitively, "British?" We nodded and she said something to this giant. He nodded and she (who was about three times my size) shouted at us, "20,000000 lira or vamoose!" We vamoosed. We ended up in Pompeii just looking at the positions that they had got up to. We realised we had to wait until we got down the gut, back in Malta, before the aching could be relieved. To think that for a twenty packet of Players cigarettes you could, in Kyrenia or Niscosia, Cyprus, have your relief any way you wanted. The same in Malta, down the gut. 20,000000 lira was about 19 and a half million more than what we had amongst the three of us. So much for Naples!

Time came for us to board the launches and head back to the *Reggio*. Before lights out we spoke to some of the other lads and not one of the marines who were in the same mind as we three were and who went ashore in Naples (a lot didn't) got any relief. American forces that sometimes visited the no-go areas had a lot more money and had set the relief ceiling too high for us Brits.

"Jammy nowts!"

86   Royal Marines 1955–1957

On shore leave in Naples

Top left: 'Tich' Cramner and I.
Top right: Bob Stroud, myself, and 'Tich' Cramner.
Centre left: Me and 'Tich' Cramner.
Centre right: Me and Bob Stroud.
Bottom: The three of us with Mount Vesuvius in the background. Naples was a very clean city, we thought.

HOMEWARD VOYAGE

The *Reggio* weighed anchor and headed south for Malta. The Med was again like a millpond. As far as I could gather from matelots, the Med does not have a tide, which means it stays at the same level nearly all of the time; that's why it is always like a millpond. The only time it gets rough is when there are storms about. This apparently has something to do with the Atlantic going past Gibraltar and Morocco and not entering the Mediterranean, I think.

We sailed, once again, into Malta's grand harbour. We disembarked, climbed into trucks and, for the last time, made our way to St. George's barracks. Once settled in, we were informed that all the lads due for demob would be shipped home to Southampton on the *H.M. Troopship Empire Fowey*. We were looking forward to this but first there was going to be a big parade for the first Lord of the Admiralty to congratulate us on our achievements at Port Said. He was to dish out a couple of medals to two of our N. C .O.s.

On the day of the parade (a Saturday) he inspected a guard of honour, the regimental colours, and stopped and spoke to one or two marines on parade. He then presented the long service medal to colour Sergeant Emerson and good conduct medal to colour Sergeant Ridout, both of 40 commando. This was done with all of the pomp you could think of, including the band of the royal marines. Why he didn't stop and speak to me I'll never know. It all went off like an occasion like this should do, great. All this over and done with, our thoughts were now of demobilisation. There were about 2000 troops from all regiments returning to 'Blighty' on board the *Empire Fowey*, some for demob and some just going on another tour of duty. We left Grand Harbour and sailed west from Malta to Gibraltar, enjoying watching the dolphins and flying fish at the bow of this enormous troopship. At night some of us slept on deck, in sleeping bags of course. Again, the Med was as flat as a pancake. We came up to the mouth of the Mediterranean with Gibraltar on our starboard bow. Gibraltar looked really formidable. The tannoy came on and announced that we would be entering the Straits of Gibraltar at about 8 p.m. We now had Spain on our starboard and Morocco on our port side. We sailed past Cape Trafalgar and up through the Gulf of Cadiz, all to starboard, with the Atlantic Ocean to our port. Up until now the voyage was going well with calm waters. We passed Cape Vincent and steered north up towards the Bay of Biscay. On the way we saw the lights of Portugal. The captain came on the tannoy and announced that we would be in the Bay of Biscay around midday, the next day. This aroused a little bit of worry as Biscay was noted for rough seas. Luckily I was okay on board a ship and had never been, or felt, seasick before, but the Bay of Biscay was reputed to be something else.

We sailed up the Portuguese coast past Porto, Vigo and A'Coruna and into the Bay of Biscay. The sea was as calm as can be. Right up to Brest on the French coast it was really calm. The tannoy came on again and announced that we would enter the English Channel at about 7 a.m. the next morning. The matelots were smiling and saying that the sea had been good to them this voyage and the worst part was over.

But they were wrong. I've never witnessed anything like the power of the sea in the Channel; it was horrendous and very frightening. For the next two days we were in peril on the sea. Without a word of a lie the swells were about 30 yards up and 30 yards down. The tannoy announced that everyone had to get below decks for safety reasons. There were people vomiting everywhere, the sickbay was full and those who couldn't get there were given pills and ordered to their bunks or hammocks. I was lucky—I was blessed with sea legs, along with quite a few other marines. When we looked out of the porthole window we could see the swells coming towards the ship: it was like a toy boat going up and down these huge swells. Just imagine a ship of that size being tossed around like a paper boat! Naturally the ship had to ride these monsters head on and we could feel the ship going up on the swell and crashing down into the troughs. We were all going to be glad when this voyage was over. The non-swimmers were the most worried, although, if the ship had capsized or sunk, I don't think anyone would have survived. The statement "You'll swim if you have to" didn't reassure us non-swimmers at all. I must admit though that the captain of the *Empire Fowey* kept reassuring all on board that everything was okay and we would soon be through these rough waters.

DEMOB

He was right, of course! After about four and a half hours we were through the worst and on our way to the Solent.

It was good to see the Isle of Wight on our starboard and we knew we would be docking at Southampton within a few hours. When we did dock and disembark, we were assembled and ordered into trucks (probably the same trucks that had picked us up at Exeter station) to proceed to Royal Marine barracks at Plymouth. It was early November 1957 and the day of demob was only nine days away. Naturally we were looking forward to this.

Looking back over this two-year adventure, I thought about the fact that in Civvy Street we would never have had the chance to see the places and things we had seen. We had been to Malta twice, Cyprus twice, North Africa, Egypt, Sardinia, Naples, Pompeii, Gozo and Comino, had sailed all over the Mediterranean, and sailed from Malta to Southampton. We had visited towns such as Valletta, Paphos, Limassol, Larnaca, Niscosia, Kyrenia, Famagusta, had invaded Port Said, went skiing on Cyprus's Mount Olympus, stood in awe at Mount Vesuvius and Pompeii. We had also seen death in Cyprus and Port Said, all in two years national service, an adventure if ever there was one. I would recommend that if you are looking for excitement, join the Royal Marines; young men need not fear joining as the marines look after you.

In barracks at Plymouth we were in the last day of service. I was on jankers for something I did—I can't remember what it was! The sergeant said, "Marine 132049, you won't be going home today as you must finish your jankers." I was looking out of a window at the lads who were to be demobbed waiting for a truck to take them to the station to get their appropriate trains when the sergeant put his head round the door and said, "Get down to the sickbay for an x-ray and join the rest of the lads getting demobbed. You've got half an hour."

Waiting for demobilisation at Plymouth Barracks, November 1957: 'Barnsley Pal', Author, 'Smudger Smith'—the end of the 2-year adventure.

"Thanks Sarge," I said and sprinted to my bed, picked up my gear, ran down the stairs, gave my gear to one of the lads and said, "I've got to get an x-ray and I'm with you—don't let the truck go without me!" I ran down to the sickbay, which was full of matelots and marines, saw the receptionist and informed him I was being demobbed and had to have an x-ray quickly. I sat down amongst the rest and hoped I was not going to have to wait long. After about five minutes a navy doctor put his head around the door and looked at me and asked, "Pulmograph?" I said straight out, "No, x-ray." The whole place erupted in laughter and I felt daft. The doctor signalled for me to go in and explained to me that a pulmograph *was* an x-ray. My face was as red as beetroot as I hurried through the full sick bay. They were still laughing and I felt like a twit. I joined the rest of the lads on the truck and never said anything about this.

We arrived at the station and shook hands and said goodbye to each other. I and 'Smudger' Smith, Jimmy Shade and Jock Miller were to be together till the train reached York, which is where Smudger got off. I got off at Newcastle and said 'so long' to Jimmy and Jock who, being Scots, were heading for Edinburgh. I've never seen any of that batch of national servicemen again. I haven't even seen the three or four Geordie regulars either. The adventure was over and it was back to reality. I reached my in-laws and knocked on the door. It was opened by my wife with my first son in her arms.

We now have two sons and two daughters who are all married and we are now the proud grandparents of one grandson and six granddaughters.

Can't be that bad eh?

MEMORIES

Of all the memories I can recollect that are not in this two-year adventure, the one of three prominent memories that readily comes to mind is of course the birth of my son Richard on the 30th December 1956 while I was in Malta—fantastic news, that was.

Another memory was the arrival of a parcel from Annie McKeag, the elderly lady who lived next door to my parents. The parcel consisted of plenty paper and cardboard and a stale loaf of bread that fell to bits on handling and revealed a half bottle of whisky. What a great lady! Jimmy Shade and I really enjoyed that drink. Sadly, Annie is dead now but I will never forget her and that parcel—tremendous stuff. We were, at the time, based at Pinetree Camp on Mount Olympus in the snow. The whisky went down a treat.

The author   *Jimmy Shade*

Jimmy Shade and I enjoying the half bottle of whisky I had received from Annie McKeag in a parcel sent from the U.K. What a lady! This great memory will never be forgotten for the rest of the time I have left on this planet!

The third memory has to be the camaraderie of all the marines I met in the two-year adventure. Below are some of their names:

Captain Grant (a hero)
C.P.L. Dann (regulars)
Mick Kelly (regulars)
Jock Hunter (regulars)
Taffy Hughes (regulars)
Sgt. Potter (regulars)
Geordie Kell (regulars)
Shags Moorcroft (regulars)
Geordie O'Neil (regulars)
Andy Wallace (regulars)
Geordie Cox (regulars)
C.P.L. Billett (regulars)
Tony Davie (regulars)
L/C. P.L. Mick Prendergast (regulars)

Terry Dungworth (regulars)
Del Lane (regulars)
Ginger Raikes (regulars)
Lt. Haynes (a hero)
'Mugsy' Martin (regulars)
Manny Mercer (regulars)
Paddy Armstrong (regulars)
Terry Jones (regulars)
C.P.L. Brian Bellas (regulars)
Lieut Preston (regulars)
'Smudger' Smith (N/Service)
Jock Miller (N/Service)
Jimmy Shade (N/Service)
Slim Wooden (N/Service)
'Yorky' Cramncr (N/Service)
'Jacko' Jackson (N/Service)
Rog Davis (N/Service)
Bob Stroud (N/Service)
Ginger Hoar (N/Service)
Tich Bradley (N/Service)
Mick Gurton (N/Service)
'Big Cockney' (N/Service)
Lt. Russell Polden (N/Service)
'Barnsley Pal' (N/Service)
The Twins (N/Service)

If your name is not on this list, I apologise—the memory is not so good nowadays! I would like to think you are all okay.

R. Lofthouse MNE. 132049

978-0-595-43589-0
0-595-43589-0